MODERN POETS
Two

Modern Poets
‑TWO‑

edited by

JIM HUNTER

Senior English Master
Bristol Grammar School

FABER AND FABER
3 Queen Square
London

First published in 1968
by Faber and Faber Limited
3 Queen Square London WC1
Reprinted 1970 and 1974
Printed in Great Britain by
Whitstable Litho Whitstable Kent

ISBN 0 571 08951 8 (paper covers)
ISBN 0 571 08447 8 (hard bound edition)

CONTENTS

INTRODUCTION

This book is one of a series of four, which I really see as a single collection. In these four volumes are printed selections from twenty-two modern poets whose language is English. I have tried to pick the poets that it would be most useful to have in such a collection, but it would be rash to assert that these are the best poets of their time. Simpler to say: here are some recent poets that deserve our attention. Choosing them was not easy. The omission I most regret is that of the Scots poet Hugh MacDiarmid, a controversial figure but one of the most interesting this century: it was felt that the Lallans in which his best work is written would stand too much in the way of readers of this anthology.

Poets are printed here in order of their date of birth. This seemed sounder than attempting to group them according to patterns which not all readers might accept.

More space has been given to some poets than to others. This should not be seen as crude value-judgement—some poets (e.g. D. H. Lawrence) are more discursive than others (e.g. Wallace Stevens). It is true, of course, that where a poet is given an unusual amount of space this is because he seems to me to offer a wide range of distinguished writing, which should be represented as fairly as possible.

There is still more apparent unfairness in the amount of notes supplied for different poets. But this, too, is not in itself a comment on the merit or interest of the poets:

some modern writers are straightforward, others are difficult. The space for notes in these books has been kept down, in order to print plenty of poetry; and the notes have had to be confined largely to necessary explanation of difficulties, though I have tried to suggest some critical approaches, and have asked one or two questions to keep the reader awake.

In writing the notes I have, of course, drawn freely on various critical works, biographies and commentaries. The notes are intended to be simple and minimal; and anyone seriously studying the poets will need to read about their work and lives for himself. In choosing poets and poems, and in writing the notes, I have been helped by conversation with a number of friends, and in particular by Frank Beecroft, Bill Haxworth, Fred Inglis and Andor Gomme.

D. H. Lawrence

Lawrence was born in 1885, the son of a Nottinghamshire coal-miner. For a short time he was a schoolteacher, then he spent the rest of his life writing and travelling with his wife Frieda. He died in 1930, in the South of France.

Lawrence's finest literary achievement was probably in his novels; but all his work is distinguished by an extraordinary originality. Vitality, spontaneity, honesty—all these are important elements in it: Lawrence is too powerful a personality to take indirect or artificial routes. Formal conventions of writing he found hampering: his best work occurs when he takes off along his own course, discovering it as he goes.

Most of Lawrence's poetry, then, is written in 'free verse': he was an intense admirer of the nineteenth-century American Walt Whitman, whose influence is the only one clearly apparent in his work. Lawrence is one of the most successful of free verse writers, because, while temperamentally he needed the suddenness and colloquialism which free verse allows, he also had a strong instinct towards incantation. Rhythm and repetition, the pulse of poetry, are insistent in all Lawrence's writing, in his novels and letters as well as in his verse.

The poems printed here do not need much comment. Lawrence's disconcerting honesty makes itself often felt, both where he lays himself humbly, vulnerably open, and where he barks his disgust at the Bourgeois. This alone would make him a memorable poet. But in addition we have the superb Lawrentian vividness of language—words simple, not 'literary', and astonishingly right: look at the descriptions of the kangaroo, or the snake, or the storm in the Black Forest.

Piano

Softly, in the dusk, a woman is singing to me
Taking me back down the vista of years, till I see
A child sitting under the piano, in the boom of the
    tingling strings
And pressing the small, poised feet of a mother who
    smiles as she sings.

In spite of myself, the insidious mastery of song
Betrays me back, till the heart of me weeps to belong
To the old Sunday evenings at home, with winter
    outside
And hymns in the cosy parlour, the tinkling piano our
    guide.

So now it is vain for the singer to burst into clamour
With the great black piano appassionato. The glamour
Of childish days is upon me, my manhood is cast
Down in the flood of remembrance, I weep like a child
    for the past.

The Best of School

The blinds are drawn because of the sun,
And the boys and the room in a colourless gloom
Of underwater float: bright ripples run
Across the walls as the blinds are blown
To let the sunlight in; and I,
As I sit on the shores of the class, alone,
Watch the boys in their summer blouses
As they write, their round heads busily bowed:
And one after another rouses
His face to look at me,
To ponder very quietly,
As seeing, he does not see.

And then he turns again, with a little, glad
Thrill of his work he turns again from me,
Having found what he wanted, having got what
     was to be had.

And very sweet it is, while the sunlight waves
In the ripening morning, to sit alone with the class
And feel the stream of awakening ripple and pass
From me to the boys, whose brightening souls it
     laves
For this little hour.

                    This morning, sweet it is
To feel the lads' looks light on me,
Then back in a swift, bright flutter to work;
Each one darting away with his
Discovery, like birds that steal and flee.

Touch after touch I feel on me
As their eyes glance at me for the grain
Of rigour they taste delightedly.

As tendrils reach out yearningly,
Slowly rotate till they touch the tree
That they cleave unto, and up which they climb
Up to their lives—so they to me.

I feel them cling and cleave to me
As vines going eagerly up; they twine
My life with other leaves, my time
Is hidden in theirs, their thrills are mine.

Kangaroo

In the northern hemisphere
Life seems to leap at the air, or skim under the wind
Like stags on rocky ground, or pawing horses, or
    springy scut-tailed rabbits.

Or else rush horizontal to charge at the sky's horizon,
Like bulls or bisons or wild pigs.

Or slip like water slippery towards its ends,
As foxes, stoats, and wolves, and prairie dogs.

Only mice, and moles, and rats, and badgers, and
    beavers, and perhaps bears
Seem belly-plumbed to the earth's mid-navel.
Or frogs that when they leap come flop, and flop to the
    centre of the earth.

But the yellow antipodal Kangaroo, when she sits up,
Who can unseat her, like a liquid drop that is heavy,
    and just touches earth.

The downward drip
The down-urge.
So much denser than cold-blooded frogs.

Delicate mother Kangaroo
Sitting up there rabbit-wise, but huge, plump-weighted,
And lifting her beautiful slender face, oh, so much more
    gently and finely lined than a rabbit's, or than a
    hare's,
Lifting her face to nibble at a round white peppermint
    drop which she loves, sensitive mother Kangaroo.

Her sensitive, long, pure-bred face.
Her full antipodal eyes, so dark,
So big and quiet and remote, having watched so many
    empty dawns in silent Australia.

Her little loose hands, and drooping Victorian shoulders.
And then her great weight below the waist, her vast pale
    belly
With a thin young yellow little paw hanging out, and
    straggle of a long thin ear, like ribbon,
Like a funny trimming to the middle of her belly, thin
    little dangle of an immature paw, and one thin ear.

Her belly, her big haunches
And, in addition, the great muscular python-stretch of
    her tail.

There, she shan't have any more peppermint drops.
So she wistfully, sensitively sniffs the air, and then turns,
    goes off in slow sad leaps
On the long flat skis of her legs,
Steered and propelled by that steel-strong snake of a
    tail.
Stops again, half turns, inquisitive to look back.
While something stirs quickly in her belly, and a lean
    little face comes out, as from a window,
Peaked and a bit dismayed,
Only to disappear again quickly away from the sight of
    the world, to snuggle down in the warmth,
Leaving the trail of a different paw hanging out.

Still she watches with eternal, cocked wistfulness!
How full her eyes are, like the full, fathomless, shining
    eyes of an Australian black-boy

Who has been lost so many centuries on the margins of
    existence!
She watches with insatiable wistfulness.
Untold centuries of watching for something to come,
For a new signal from life, in that silent lost land of
    the South.

Where nothing bites but insects and snakes and the sun,
    small life,
Where no bull roared, no cow ever lowed, no stag cried,
    no leopard screeched, no lion coughed, no dog
    barked,
But all was silent save for parrots occasionally, in the
    haunted blue bush.

Wistfully watching, with wonderful liquid eyes.
And all her weight, all her blood, dripping sack-wise
    down towards the earth's centre,
And the live little-one taking in its paw at the door of
    her belly.

Leap then, and come down on the line that draws to the
    earth's deep, heavy centre.

Sydney

Snake

A snake came to my water-trough
On a hot, hot day, and I in pyjamas for the heat,
To drink there.

In the deep, strange-scented shade of the great dark
    carob-tree
I came down the steps with my pitcher
And must wait, must stand and wait, for there he was
    at the trough before me.

He reached down from a fissure in the earth-wall in the
    gloom
And trailed his yellow-brown slackness soft-bellied
    down, over the edge of the stone trough
And rested his throat upon the stone bottom,
And where the water had dripped from the tap, in a
    small clearness,
He sipped with his straight mouth,
Softly drank through his straight gums, into his slack
    long body,
Silently.

Someone was before me at my water-trough,
And I, like a second comer, waiting.

He lifted his head from his drinking, as cattle do,
And looked at me vaguely, as drinking cattle do,
And flickered his two-forked tongue from his lips, and
    mused a moment,
And stooped and drank a little more,

Being earth-brown, earth-golden from the burning
    bowels of the earth
On the day of Sicilian July, with Etna smoking.

The voice of my education said to me
He must be killed,
For in Sicily the black, black snakes are innocent, the
    gold are venomous.

And voices in me said, If you were a man
You would take a stick and break him now, and finish
    him off.

But must I confess how I liked him,
How glad I was he had come like a guest in quiet, to
    drink at my water-trough
And depart peaceful, pacified, and thankless,
Into the burning bowels of this earth.

Was it cowardice, that I dared not kill him?
Was it perversity, that I longed to talk to him?
Was it humility, to feel so honoured?
I felt so honoured.

And yet those voices!
If you were not afraid, you would kill him!

And truly I was afraid, I was most afraid,
But even so, honoured still more
That he should seek my hospitality
From out the dark door of the secret earth.

He drank enough
And lifted his head, dreamily, as one who has drunken,

And flickered his tongue like a forked night on the air, so
     black,
Seeming to lick his lips,
And looked around like a god, unseeing, into the air,
And slowly turned his head,
And slowly, very slowly, as if thrice adream,
Proceeded to draw his slow length curving round
And climb again the broken bank of my wall-face.

And as he put his head into that dreadful hole,
And as he slowly drew up, snake-easing his shoulders,
     and entered farther,
A sort of horror, a sort of protest against his with-
     drawing into that horrid black hole,
Deliberately going into the blackness, and slowly
     drawing himself after,
Overcame me now his back was turned.

I looked round, I put down my pitcher,
I picked up a clumsy log
And threw it at the water-trough with a clatter.

I think it did not hit him,
But suddenly that part of him that was left behind
     convulsed in undignified haste,
Writhed like lightning, and was gone
Into the black hole, the earth-lipped fissure in the
     wall-front,
At which, in the intense still noon, I stared with
     fascination.

And immediately I regretted it.
I thought how paltry, how vulgar, what a mean act!

I despised myself and the voices of my accursed
    human education.
And I thought of the albatross,
And I wished he would come back, my snake.

For he seemed to me again like a king,
Like a king in exile, uncrowned in the underworld,
Now due to be crowned again.

And so, I missed my chance with one of the lords
Of life.
And I have something to expiate;
A pettiness.

Taormina

Storm in the Black Forest

Now it is almost night, from the bronzey soft sky
jugful after jugful of pure white liquid fire, bright
    white
tipples over and spills down,
and is gone
and gold-bronze flutters beat through the thick upper
    air.
And as the electric liquid pours out, sometimes
a still brighter white snake wriggles among it, spilled
and tumbling wriggling down the sky:
and then the heavens crackle with uncouth sounds.

And the rain won't come, the rain refuses to come!

This is the electricity that man is supposed to have
    mastered
chained, subjugated to his use!
supposed to!

Song of a Man who is Loved

Between her breasts is my home, between her breasts.
Three sides set on me space and fear, but the fourth side
    rests
Sure and a tower of strength, 'twixt the walls of her
    breasts.

Having known the world so long, I have never confessed
How it impresses me, how hard and compressed
Rocks seem, and earth, and air uneasy, and waters still
    ebbing west.

All things on the move, going their own little ways, and
    all
Jostling, people touching and talking and making small
Contacts and bouncing off again, bounce! bounce like a
    ball!

My flesh is weary with bounce and gone again!—
My ears are weary with words that bounce on them, and
    then
Bounce off again, meaning nothing. Assertions!
    Assertions! stones, women and men!

Between her breasts is my home, between her breasts.
Three sides set on me chaos and bounce, but the fourth
    side rests
Sure on a haven of peace, between the mounds of her
    breasts.

I am that I am, and no more than that: but so much
I am, nor will I be bounced out of it. So at last I touch
All that I am-not in softness, sweet softness, for she is
    such.

And the chaos that bounces and rattles like shrapnel, at
     least
Has for me a door into peace, warm dawn in the east
Where her bosom softens towards me, and the turmoil
     has eased.

So I hope I shall spend eternity
With my face down buried between her breasts;
And my still heart full of security,
And my still hands full of her breasts.

Bavarian Gentians

Not every man has gentians in his house
in Soft September, at slow, Sad Michaelmas.

Bavarian gentians, big and dark, only dark
darkening the day-time torch-like with the smoking
     blueness of Pluto's gloom,
ribbed and torch-like, with their blaze of darkness
     spread blue
down flattening into points, flattened under the sweep of
     white day
torch-flower of the blue-smoking darkness, Pluto's
     dark-blue daze,
black lamps from the halls of Dio, burning dark blue,
giving off darkness, blue darkness, as Demeter's pale
     lamps give off light,
lead me then, lead me the way.

Reach me a gentian, give me a torch
let me guide myself with the blue, forked torch of this
      flower
down the darker and darker stairs, where blue is darkened
      on blueness.
even where Persephone goes, just now, from the frosted
      September
to the sightless realm where darkness is awake upon the
      dark
and Persephone herself is but a voice
or a darkness invisible enfolded in the deeper dark
of the arms of Plutonic, and pierced with the passion of
      dense gloom,
among the splendour of torches of darkness, shedding
      darkness on the lost bride and her groom.

Red Geranium and Godly Mignonette

Imagine that any mind ever *thought* a red geranium!
As if the redness of a red geranium could be anything
    but a sensual experience
And as if sensual experience could take place before
    there were any senses.
We know that even God could not imagine the redness
    of a red geranium
nor the smell of mignonette
when geraniums were not, and mignonette neither.
And even when they were, even God would have to have
    a nose
to smell at the mignonette.
You can't imagine the Holy Ghost sniffing at cherry-pie
    heliotrope,
Or the Most High, during the coal age, cudgelling his
    mighty brains
even if he had any brains: straining his mighty mind
to think, among the moss and mud of lizards and
    mastodons
to think out, in the abstract, when all was twilit green
    and muddy:
'Now there shall be tum-tiddly-um, and tum-tiddly-um,
hey presto! scarlet geranium!'

We know it couldn't be done.

But imagine, among the mud and the mastodons
God sighing and yearning with tremendous creative
    yearning, in that dark green mess
oh, for some other beauty, some other beauty
that blossomed at last, red geranium, and mignonette.

How Beastly the Bourgeois Is

How beastly the bourgeois is
especially the male of the species—

Presentable, eminently presentable—
shall I make you a present of him?

Isn't he handsome? isn't he healthy? Isn't he a fine
    specimen?
doesn't he look the fresh clean englishman, outside?
Isn't it god's own image? tramping his thirty miles a
    day
after partridges, or a little rubber ball?
wouldn't you like to be like that, well off, and quite the
    thing?

Oh, but wait!
Let him meet a new emotion, let him be faced with
    another man's need,
let him come home to a bit of moral difficulty, let life
    face him with a new demand on his understanding
and then watch him go soggy, like a wet meringue.
Watch him turn into a mess, either a fool or a bully.
Just watch the display of him, confronted with a new
    demand on his intelligence,
a new life-demand.

How beastly the bourgeois is
especially the male of the species—

Nicely groomed, like a mushroom
standing there so sleek and erect and eyeable—

and like a fungus, living on the remains of bygone life
sucking his life out of the dead leaves of greater life than
    his own.

And even so, he's stale, he's been there too long.
Touch him, and you'll find he's all gone inside
just like an old mushroom, all wormy inside, and
    hollow
under a smooth skin and an upright appearance.

Full of seething, wormy, hollow feelings
rather nasty—
How beastly the bourgeois is!

Standing in their thousands, these appearances, in damp
    England
what a pity they can't all be kicked over
like sickening toadstools, and left to melt back, swiftly
into the soil of England.

In Trouble and Shame

I look at the swaling sunset
   And wish I could go also
Through the red doors beyond the black-purple bar.

   I wish that I could go
Through the red doors where I could put off
   My shame like shoes in the porch,
   My pain like garments,
And leave my flesh discarded lying
Like luggage of some departed traveller
   Gone one knows not whither.

   Then I would turn round,
And seeing my cast-off body lying like lumber,
   I would laugh with joy.

Song of a Man who has Come Through

Not I, not I, but the wind that blows through me!
A fine wind is blowing the new direction of Time.
If only I let it bear me, carry me, if only it carry me!
If only I am sensitive, subtle, oh, delicate, a winged gift!
If only, most lovely of all, I yield myself and am
    borrowed
By the fine, fine wind that takes its course through the
    chaos of the world
Like a fine, an exquisite chisel, a wedge-blade inserted;
If only I am keen and hard like the sheer tip of a wedge
Driven by invisible blows,
The rock will split, we shall come at the wonder, we
    shall find the Hesperides.

Oh, for the wonder that bubbles into my soul,
I would be a good fountain, a good well-head,
Would blur no whisper, spoil no expression.

What is the knocking?
What is the knocking at the door in the night?
It is somebody wants to do us harm.

No, no, it is the three strange angels.
Admit them, admit them.

Notes

PIANO

A courageous, direct tackling of an old artistic problem. Lawrence dislikes sentimentality: the first verse is, in its muzzy glow, not typical of him (though the exact detail of 'the boom of the tingling strings' gives the lines a feeling of realism). The opening of the second verse makes his disapproval explicit: 'in spite of myself . . . insidious . . . Betrays me. . .'. But, for all its impropriety, the emotion is *real*, and it is thoroughly characteristic of Lawrence that he ends by honestly acknowledging and expressing it.

THE BEST OF SCHOOL

Lawrence was, we are told, a superb teacher, where he was free of discipline troubles. This poem shows clearly enough why. He responded intensely to whatever was alive; and not only to a crude, blazing vitality, but also to tentative, fluid, sensitive life such as that of children, or of the 'delicate mother Kangaroo'. The poem goes characteristically straight to the heart of what 'the best of school' is, or should be. No teacher's autobiography or academic novel achieves anything like this clear-eyed understanding.

SNAKE

The conflict between Lawrence's instinctive sympathy towards the snake and 'the voice of my education' is a fundamental theme of all his work. 'What our blood feels and believes and says is always true. The intellect is only a bit and a bridle.'

Be sure you understand the word 'expiate', and its appropriateness to the Sicilian landscape, the snake 'like a god', the volcano smoking, and 'a king in exile'. The albatross has always been regarded as a bird it is dangerous to molest; you may remember *The Ancient Mariner* of Coleridge.

BAVARIAN GENTIANS

An unusually 'literary' poem for Lawrence; but this classical Underworld is alive and freshly-imagined, not straight out of books. Lawrence's feeling for ritual and incantation is very apparent here.

The poem has little force unless one knows what gentians are.

HOW BEASTLY THE BOURGEOIS IS

A bourgeois is a self-satisfied member of the middle-class. The breed has thinned out a bit and changed its colouring slightly since Lawrence's day; but not all that much.

What do the last lines suggest about Lawrence's feelings towards England, as distinct from bourgeois Englishmen?

IN TROUBLE AND SHAME

'Swaling' means burning.

SONG OF A MAN WHO HAS COME THROUGH

The Hesperides, in mythology, were the gardens of paradise at the edge of the world.

This is a difficult and perhaps rather private poem. It was important to Lawrence, I think; and his wife took from it the title of her autobiography *Not I, But The Wind*. I don't know who the 'three strange angels' are, and the exact subject-matter of the poem cannot be fixed; but the emotional statement is fairly clear, and consistent with Lawrence's other work. In the 'chaos of the world' there *is* wonder, a fine wind does blow; and Lawrence himself can, at his best, be a vehicle for that wonder, especially when he surrenders himself to it. The 'three strange angels' presumably represent the sort of visitation of wonder which can be experienced by a man who has come through.

34

Ezra Pound

Ezra Pound was born in 1885 in Idaho, and brought up in Philadelphia. He studied and taught literature and languages in American universities before coming to Europe in 1908. Until 1920 he lived in London, publishing poems and criticism, meeting, haranguing, and frequently helping many writers and artists, including W. B. Yeats (whose early poetry Pound was influenced by, and whose later poetry Pound had an influence on), James Joyce, and T. S. Eliot. Arrogant and wrong Pound may often have been, but it is clear that he was also a person of tremendous energy and generosity and an ebullient exploratory mind: 'curiosity' is one of the magic words to Pound. Between 1921 and 1925 he lived in Paris; in 1925 he moved to Rapallo in Italy. He became a sympathizer with Italian fascism and made propaganda broadcasts on Italian radio during the Second World War, for which he was arrested by American troops in 1945. He was found insane and committed to an asylum. In 1958 he was released, and he now lives again in Italy.

Since 1920 Pound has worked on a huge linked series of poems called the CANTOS, and (as at all times in his career) on translations, especially from Chinese. The CANTOS are intended to be in the tradition of the long epic poem, but their subject is human civilizations and their structure is not that of coherent narrative. Pound certainly regarded them, as do many critics, as his great work; but they are exceedingly difficult, and in the present selection I have more or less evaded them by including only CANTO XVII, an early and deservedly well-known descriptive piece.

Pound is one of the most 'literary' poets ever. Poetry for

35

him is not a means for simple emotion or meditation. It is a craft: the hammering out of words into lines, where precision and directness combine with a sense of the great poetry of the past. It is an irony of the twentieth-century that an American (whose country many people, as Pound bitterly records, regarded as 'half-savage') should be the most persistent voice persuading us to renew our contact with ancient culture. Part of Pound's intention, especially in his later work, is, indeed, to educate us, to make us read other poets and philosophers, especially those of classical China and Japan.

Imitation of earlier poetry, a completely respectable activity in, say, seventeenth- or eighteenth-century England, is again made respectable by Pound. And it is as creative imitation that his translations also can be seen: they are often inaccurate as scholarly translations, sometimes in places where Pound must have known how he was departing from the original, but they are consistent and distinguished poems in their own right.

Pound is widely regarded as the finest verse-writer of the century; where the tendency of many modern poets, reasonably and successfully, is to write a loose rhythm of stresses and irregular numbers of light syllables, Pound is always sensitive to each individual syllable; and although his verse is not often 'regular' in ancient metrical systems, it achieves an extraordinary poise. Syllables are not shuffled clumsily in where there is not quite room for them; and the verse-line, to Pound, is a separate unit as it had hardly been in English poetry for centuries—see how little enjambement there is between lines in CANTO XVII or HUGH SELWYN MAUBERLEY. In this technical achievement as in so many other aspects of his work, Pound succeeds in rediscovering and reviving the greatness of the past.

Ballad o' the Goodly Fere

Simon Zelotes speaketh it somewhile after the Crucifixion

Ha' we lost the goodliest fere o' all
For the priests and the gallows tree?
Aye lover he was of brawny men,
O' ships and the open sea.

When they came wi' a host to take Our Man
His smile was good to see.
'First let these go!' quo' our Goodly Fere,
'Or I'll see ye damned,' says he.

Aye he sent us out through the crossed high spears
And the scorn of his laugh rang free,
'Why took ye not me when I walked about
Alone in the town?' says he.

Oh we drunk his 'Hale' in the good red wine
When we last made company,
No capon priest was the Goodly Fere
But a man o' men was he.

I ha' seen him drive a hundred men
Wi' a bundle o' cords swung free,
That they took the high and holy house
For their pawn and treasury.

They'll no' get him a' in a book I think
Though they write it cunningly;
No mouse of the scrolls was the Goodly Fere
But aye loved the open sea.

If they think they ha' snared our Goodly Fere
They are fools to the last degree.
'I'll go to the feast,' quo' our Goodly Fere,
'Though I go to the gallows tree.'

'Ye ha' seen me heal the lame and blind,
And wake the dead,' says he.
'Ye shall see one thing to master all:
'Tis how a brave man dies on the tree.'

A son of God was the Goodly Fere
That bade us his brothers be.
I ha' seen him cow a thousand men.
I have seen him upon the tree.

He cried no cry when they drave the nails
And the blood gushed hot and free,
The hounds of the crimson sky gave tongue
But never a cry cried he.

I ha' seen him cow a thousand men
On the hills o' Galilee,
They whined as he walked out calm between,
Wi' his eyes like the grey o' the sea,

Like the sea that brooks no voyaging
With the winds unleashed and free,
Like the sea that he cowed at Genseret
Wi' twey words spoke suddently.

A master of men was the Goodly Fere,
A mate of the wind and sea,

If they think they ha' slain our Goodly Fere
They are fools eternally.

I ha' seen him eat o' the honey-comb
Sin' they nailed him to the tree.

An Immorality

Sing we for love and idleness,
Naught else is worth the having.

Though I have been in many a land,
There is naught else in living.

And I would rather have my sweet,
Though rose-leaves die of grieving,

Than do high deeds in Hungary
To pass all men's believing.

The Seafarer

from the Anglo-Saxon

May I for my own self song's truth reckon,
Journey's jargon, how I in harsh days
Hardship endured oft.
Bitter breast-cares have I abided,
Known on my keel many a care's hold,
And dire sea-surge, and there I oft spent
Narrow nightwatch nigh the ship's head
While she tossed close to cliffs. Coldly afflicted,
My feet were by frost benumbed.
Chill its chains are; chafing sighs
Hew my heart round and hunger begot
Mere-weary mood. Lest man know not
That he on dry land loveliest liveth,
List how I, care-wretched, on ice-cold sea,
Weathered the winter, wretched outcast
Deprived of my kinsmen;
Hung with hard ice-flakes, where hail-scur flew,
There I heard naught save the harsh sea
And ice-cold wave, at whiles the swan cries,
Did for my games the gannet's clamour,
Sea-fowls' loudness was for me laughter,
The mews' singing all my mead-drink.
Storms, on the stone-cliffs beaten, fell on the stern
In icy feathers; full oft the eagle screamed
With spray on his pinion.

                              Not any protector
May make merry man faring needy.
This he little believes, who aye in winsome life
Abides 'mid burghers some heavy business,
Wealthy and wine-flushed, how I weary oft

Must bide above brine.
Neareth nightshade, snoweth from north,
Frost froze the land, hail fell on earth then,
Corn of the coldest. Nathless there knocketh now
The heart's thought that I on high streams
The salt-wavy tumult traverse alone.
Moaneth alway my mind's lust
That I fare forth, that I afar hence
Seek out a foreign fastness.
For this there's no mood-lofty man over earth's
     midst,
Not though he be given his good, but will have in his
     youth greed;
Nor his deed to the daring, nor his king to the faithful
But shall have his sorrow for sea-fare
Whatever his lord will.
He hath not heart for harping, nor in ring-having
Nor winsomeness to wife, nor world's delight
Nor any whit else save the wave's slash,
Yet longing comes upon him to fare forth on the
     water.
Bosque taketh blossom, cometh beauty of berries,
Fields to fairness, land fares brisker,
All this admonisheth man eager of mood,
The heart turns to travel so that he then thinks
On flood-ways to be far departing.
Cuckoo calleth with gloomy crying,
He singeth summer-ward, bodeth sorrow,
The bitter heart's blood. Burgher knows not—
He the prosperous man—what some perform
Where wandering them widest draweth.
So that but now my heart burst from my breastlock,
My mood 'mid the mere-flood,
Over the whale's acre, would wander wide.

On earth's shelter cometh oft to me,
Eager and ready, the crying lone-flyer,
Whets for the whale-path the heart irresistibly,
O'er tracks of ocean; seeing that anyhow
My lord deems to me this dead life
On loan and on land, I believe not
That any earth-weal eternal standeth
Save there be somewhat calamitous
That, ere a man's tide go, turn it to twain.
Disease of oldness or sword-hate
Beats out the breath from doom-gripped body.
And for this, every earl whatever, for those speaking
    after—
Laud of the living, boasteth some last word,
That he will work ere he pass onward,
Frame on the fair earth 'gainst foes his malice,
Daring ado. . .
So that all men shall honour him after
And his laud beyond them remain 'mid the English,
Aye, for ever, a lasting life's-blast,
Delight 'mid the doughty.
                      Days little durable,
And all arrogance of earthen riches.
There come now no kings nor Caesars
Nor gold-giving lords like those gone.
Howe'er in mirth most magnified,
Whoe'er lived in life most lordliest,
Drear all this excellence, delights undurable!
Waneth the watch, but the world holdeth.
Tomb hideth trouble. The blade is layed low.
Earthly glory ageth and seareth.
No man at all going the earth's gait,
But age fares against him, his face paleth,
Grey-haired he groaneth, knows gone companions,

Lordly men, are to earth o'er given,
Nor may he then the flesh-cover, whose life ceaseth,
Nor eat the sweet nor feel the sorry,
Nor stir hand nor think in mid heart,
And though he strew the grave with gold,
His born brothers, their buried bodies
Be an unlikely treasure hoard.

Liu Ch'e

The rustling of the silk is discontinued,
Dust drifts over the court-yard,
There is no sound of footfall, and the leaves
Scurry into heaps and lie still,
And she the rejoicer of the heart is beneath them:

A wet leaf that clings to the threshold.

Ts'ai Chi'h

The petals fall in the fountain,
    the orange-coloured rose-leaves,
Their ochre clings to the stone.

In a Station of the Métro

The apparition of these faces in the crowd;
Petals on a wet, black bough.

Alba

As cool as the pale wet leaves
    of lily-of-the-valley
She lay beside me in the dawn.

Heather

The black panther treads at my side,
And above my fingers
There float the petal-like flames.

The milk-white girls
Unbend from the holly-trees,
And their snow-white leopard
Watches to follow our trace.

44

The Social Order

I

This government official
Whose wife is several years his senior,
Has such a caressing air
When he shakes hands with young ladies.

II
(Pompes Funèbres)

This old lady,
Who was 'so old that she was an atheist',
Is now surrounded
By six candles and a crucifix,
While the second wife of a nephew
Makes hay with the things in her house.
Her two cats
Go before her into Avernus;
A sort of chloroformed suttee,
And it is to be hoped that their spirits will walk
With their tails up,
And with a plaintive, gentle mewing,
For it is certain that she has left on this earth
No sound
Save a squabble of female connections.

The Beautiful Toilet

Blue, blue is the grass about the river
And the willows have overfilled the close garden.
And within, the mistress, in the midmost of her youth,
White, white of face, hesitates, passing the door.
Slender, she puts forth a slender hand;
And she was a courtesan in the old days,
And she has married a sot,
Who now goes drunkenly out
And leaves her too much alone.

by Mei Sheng 140 B.C.

The Jewel-Stairs' Grievance

The jewelled steps are already quite white with dew,
It is so late that the dew soaks my gauze stockings,
And I let down the crystal curtain
And watch the moon through the clear autumn.

by Rihaku

Separation on the River Kiang

Ko-jin goes west from Ko-kaku-ro,
The smoke-flowers are blurred over the river.
His lone sail blots the far sky.
And now I see only the river,
The long Kiang, reaching heaven.

Rihaku

Taking Leave of a Friend

Blue mountains to the north of the walls,
White river winding about them;
Here we must make separation
And go out through a thousand miles of dead grass.

Mind like a floating cloud,
Sunset like the parting of old acquaintances
Who bow over their clasped hands at a distance.
Our horses neigh to each other
                    as we are departing.

                              Rihaku

Leave-Taking Near Shoku

'Sanso, King of Shoku, built roads'

They say the roads of Sanso are steep,
Sheer as the mountains.
The walls rise in a man's face,
Clouds grow out of the hill
                    at his horse's bridle.
Sweet trees are on the paved way of the Shin,
Their trunks burst through the paving,
And freshets are bursting their ice
                    in the midst of Shoku, a proud city.

Men's fates are already set,
There is no need of asking diviners.

                              Rihaku

from *Hugh Selwyn Mauberley*

E.P. *Ode Pour L' Election de son Sepulchre*

For three years, out of key with his time,
He strove to resuscitate the dead art
Of poetry; to maintain 'the sublime'
In the old sense. Wrong from the start—

5   No, hardly, but seeing he had been born
In a half-savage country, out of date;
Bent resolutely on wringing lilies from the acorn;
Capaneus; trout for factitious bait;

     ῎Ιδμεν γάρ τοι πάνθ', ὅσ' ἐνὶ Τροίῃ
10   Caught in the unstopped ear;
Giving the rocks small lee-way
The chopped seas held him, therefore, that year.

His true Penelope was Flaubert,
He fished by obstinate isles;
15   Observed the elegance of Circe's hair
Rather than the mottoes on sundials.

Unaffected by 'the march of events,'
He passed from men's memory in *l'an trentiesme
De son eage*; the case presents
20   No adjunct to the Muses' diadem.

II

The age demanded an image
Of its accelerated grimace,

Something for the modern stage,
Not, at any rate, an Attic grace;

Not, not certainly, the obscure reveries   25
Of the inward gaze;
Better mendacities
Than the classics in paraphrase!

The 'age demanded' chiefly, a mould in plaster,
Made with no loss of time,   30
A prose kinema, not, not assuredly, alabaster
Or the 'sculpture' of rhyme.

III

The tea-rose tea-gown, etc.
Supplants the mousseline of Cos,
The pianola 'replaces'   35
Sappho's barbitos.

Christ follows Dionysus,
Phallic and ambrosial
Made way for macerations;
Caliban casts out Ariel.   40

All things are a flowing,
Sage Heracleitus says;
But a tawdry cheapness
Shall outlast our days.

Even the Christian beauty   45
Defects—after Samothrace;
We see τὸ καλὸν
Decreed in the market-place.

Faun's flesh is not to us,
Nor the saint's vision.
We have the Press for wafer;
Franchise for circumcision.

50

All men, in law, are equals.
Free of Pisistratus,
We choose a knave or an eunuch
To rule over us.

55

O bright Apollo,
τίν ἄνδρα, τίν' ἤρωα, τίνα θεὸν,
What god, man, or hero
Shall I place a tin wreath upon!

60

IV

These fought in any case
and some believing,

pro domo, in any case . . .

Some quick to arm,
some for adventure,
some from fear of weakness,
some from fear of censure,
some for love of slaughter, in imagination,
learning later . . .
some in fear, learning love of slaughter;

65

70

Died some, pro patria,

non 'dulce' non 'et decor' . . .
walked eye-deep in hell
believing in old men's lies, then unbelieving
come home, home to a lie,

75

home to many deceits,
home to old lies and new infamy;
usury age-old and age-thick
and liars in public places.

Daring as never before, wastage as never before.   80
Young blood and high blood,
fair cheeks, and fine bodies;

fortitude as never before

frankness as never before,
disillusions as never told in the old days,   85
hysterias, trench confessions,
laughter out of dead bellies.

V

There died a myriad,
And of the best, among them,
For an old bitch gone in the teeth,   90
For a botched civilization,

Charm, smiling at the good mouth,
Quick eyes gone under earth's lid,

For two gross of broken statues,
For a few thousand battered books.   95

So that the vines burst from my fingers
And the bees weighted with pollen
Move heavily in the vine-shoots:
  chirr-chirr-chir-rikk—a purring sound,
5 And the birds sleepily in the branches.
  ZAGREUS! IO ZAGREUS!
With the first pale-clear of the heaven
And the cities set in their hills,
And the goddess of the fair knees
10 Moving there, with the oak-wood behind her,
The green slope, with white hounds
    leaping about her;
And thence down to the creek's mouth, until evening,
Flat water before me,
15   and the trees growing in water,
Marble trunks out of stillness,
On past the palazzi,
    in the stillness,
The light now, not of the sun.
20   Chrysophrase,
And the water green clear, and blue clear;
On, to the great cliffs of amber.
     Between them,
Cave of Nerea,
25   she like a great shell curved,
And the boat drawn without sound,
Without odour of ship-work,
Nor bird-cry, nor any noise of wave moving,
Nor splash of porpoise, nor any noise of wave moving,
30 Within her cave, Nerea,
    she like a great shell curved

In the suavity of the rock,
                    cliff green-gray in the far,
In the near, the gate-cliffs of amber,
And the wave,   35
                green clear, and blue clear,
And the cave salt-white, and glare-purple,
                cool, porphyry smooth,
                the rock sea-worn.
No gull-cry, no sound of porpoise,   40
Sand as of malachite, and no cold there,
                the light not of the sun.

Zagreus, feeding his panthers,
                the turf clear as on hills under light.
And under the almond-trees, gods,   45
                with them, *choros nympharum*. Gods,
Hermes and Athene,
                As shaft of compass,
Between them, trembled—
To the left is the place of fauns,   50
                sylva nympharum;
The low wood, moor-scrub,
        the doe, the young spotted deer,
        leap up through the broom-plants,
                as dry leaf amid yellow.   55
And by one cut of the hills,
        the great alley of Memnons.
Beyond, sea, crests seen over dune
Night sea churning shingle,
To the left, the alley of cypress.   60
                        A boat came,
One man holding her sail,
Guiding her with oar caught over gunwale, saying:
        'There, in the forest of marble,

65   the stone trees—out of water—
            the arbours of stone—
            marble leaf, over leaf,
            silver, steel over steel,
            silver beaks rising and crossing,
70   prow set against prow,
            stone, ply over ply,
            the gilt beams flare of an evening'
Borso, Carmagnola, the men of craft, *i vitrei*,
Thither, at one time, time after time,
75   And the waters richer than glass,
Bronze gold, the blaze over the silver,
Dye-pots in the torch-light,
The flash of wave under prows,
And the silver beaks rising and crossing,
80   Stone trees, white and rose-white in the darkness,
Cypress there by the towers,
        Drift under hulls in the night.

        'In the gloom the gold
Gathers the light about it'. . .

85   Now supine in burrow, half over-arched bramble,
One eye for the sea, through that peek-hole,
Gray light, with Athene.
Zothar and her elephants, the gold loin-cloth,
The sistrum, shaken, shaken,
90   the cohort of her dancers.
And Aletha, by bend of the shore,
              with her eyes seaward,
           and in her hands sea-wrack
Salt-bright with the foam.
95   Koré through the bright meadow,
               with green-gray dust in the grass:

'For this hour, brother of Circe.'
Arm laid over my shoulder,
Saw the sun for three days, the sun fulvid,
As a lion lift over sand-plain;   100
                              and that day,
And for three days, and none after,
Splendour, as the splendour of Hermes,
And shipped thence
                              to the stone place,   105
Pale white, over water,
                              known water,
And the white forest of marble, bent bough over bough,
The pleached arbour of stone,
Thither Borso, when they shot the barbed arrow at him,   110
And Carmagnola, between the two columns,
Sigismundo, after the wreck in Dalmatia,
      Sunset like the grasshopper flying.

Notes

BALLAD O' THE GOODLY FERE
Fere means mate or comrade.

Popular early, this poem has more recently been reviled, for sentimentality and for a certain Hollywood clumsiness about the imitation of English dialects. It is still in places a powerful descendant of the traditional ballad—obviously it is a studied imitation—and it compares well with recent 'folk-songs' of the recording studios.

AN IMMORALITY
A skilful imitation of classical or medieval secular lyrics. The warm lightness is a quality which more or less dropped out of English poetry about 1700.

THE SEAFARER
A frequently inaccurate but vigorous version of an Anglo-Saxon poem. Pound was interested by the verse-form, the alliterative line with a 'heave' in the middle. Each line, itself a separate unit, is in turn divided into two. The result is a revived discipline, a recultivated sense of incantation: and these are qualities which characterize much of Pound's poetry, as well as that of his disciple T. S. Eliot.

LIU CH'E
This and the next four poems are examples of Pound's very short 'imagiste' poems, printed in *Lustra* (1916). They are influenced by the Japanese *haiku* form, very brief and concrete, not interpreted or developed. Pound said they represented 'a sort of poetry where painting or sculpture seems as it were "just coming over into speech" '.

THE SOCIAL ORDER

Imagism merges into epigram, particularly in ironic social observations such as this poem.

Avernus: Hell, the underworld: *suttee:* an allusion to the Hindu custom of burning the widow on her husband's funeral pyre; here the cat corresponds to the widow, the old lady to the husband.

THE BEAUTIFUL TOILET

This, and the following four poems, are versions from Chinese. Pound knew no Chinese at the time; his versions were based on prose scripts by Ernest Fenellosa, an American expert on Japanese art. Fenellosa's scripts were, in turn, only translations, being his Japanese rendering of the Chinese characters. (*Rihaku* is the Japanese reading of the poet's name-symbol, which in Chinese was really Li-Po.) So we do not look to Pound for accurate translations of Li-Po's poems; the value of his versions is as a fine poetic re-creation of the characteristics of Chinese poetry.

The fact that oriental poetry is 'written in pictures' makes it instinctively exclude abstraction or discursive comment. The simplicity and concreteness appealed strongly to Pound, and his versions have a delicacy which is impressive. The kinship with Imagism is clear enough.

THE JEWEL-STAIRS' GRIEVANCE

Pound's own note reads: 'Jewel stairs, therefore a palace. Grievance, therefore there is something to complain of. Gauze stockings, therefore a court lady, not a servant who complains. Clear autumn, therefore he has no excuse on account of weather. Also she has come early, for the dew has not merely whitened the stairs, but has soaked her stockings. The poem is especially prized because she utters no direct reproach.'

HUGH SELWYN MAUBERLEY

Printed here are the first five poems in HUGH SELWYN

MAUBERLEY (1920), Pound's most widely admired work outside the CANTOS. Mauberley is an imaginary poet of Pound's invention: the relationship he bears to Pound himself is variable and puzzling. As with *Personae*, Pound's collected earlier poems, the poet speaks through a variety of masks—a method of self-scrutiny and self-discovery used by two poets Pound admired: Robert Browning and W. B. Yeats. In other words, we cannot always take what the poems say as what Pound himself thought.

Ode. . . . This poem, in fact, purports to be an elegy for Pound himself (the title, incidentally, is an ironic reference to a similar poem by the French poet Ronsard). Pound presents the placing judgement which other people might feel inclined to make on him, had he died at 29—but which *he* would certainly not accept.

6. *half-savage country*: America. 7. *lilies* suggests aestheticism, fragility, uselessness. The *acorn* is something sturdier and more prosaic. 8. *Capaneus* was one of the Seven against Thebes, who was struck by Zeus's lightning when attempting to scale the city walls. As an image for E.P., his name presumably is meant to suggest futility, abortive attempt; *factitious* means here false, deluding; E.P., one might say, was 'hooked' by ideas which would lead him nowhere.

9. 'For we know all the things that are in Troy'—a line from Homer's *Odyssey*. The idea of the epic had caught Pound's imagination (the CANTOS are his epic); he realizes that this can seem to many like a fatal enchantment, and (since he has referred to the *Odyssey*) he compares it to the song of the Sirens who, in that poem, lured sailors into shipwreck.

13. *Penelope* was Odysseus's wife, to whom he ought to have been returning while he wandered among the islands. Pound, we are told, ought to have been pursuing the ideals of the French novelist Flaubert, that is, earnest self-dedication to literature. This rebuke is sarcastic: Pound is accused of neglecting his true bent, but also of having a foolish bent at

the best of times. (Flaubert was widely felt by British critics—not, of course, by Pound—to be committed overmuch to Art and not enough to Life.)

14. Instead of returning dircct to Penelope, E. P. Odysseus wandered wilfully around the islands (that is, again, he flirted with grandiose ideas of the epic). 15. *Circe*: the island enchantress who bewitched Odysseus's men. Pound was bewitched by aesthetic notions ('observed the elegance'. . .). 16. *mottoes on sundials* are good homely common sense about the passing of time and the need to act.

17–18. The French medieval poet Villon described himself as passing from sight in his thirtieth year (his words are quoted exactly, spelling and all). But (19–20) whereas Villon was a new jewel in the Muses' diadem, Pound was nothing of the sort. A flat dismissal.

II makes it clear that Pound is not really repentant, in I, of his poetic inclinations. What is wrong is not the poet, but the age.

24. *Attic*: of classical Greece.

27. *mendacities*: falsehoods.

28. Pound's *Homage to Sextus Propertius* is 'classics in paraphrase'.

31. *kinema*: cinema. The whole verse is a bitter comment on the shoddy quickly-produced social-comment art of the time: it would apply even more forcefully today. 32. *the 'sculpture' of rhyme* is a reference to the principles of the French poet Gautier whom Pound fiercely admired.

III. The ideas of II more fully developed: oh, what a wretched age we live in!

33–4. 'The tea-gown is now favoured over the fashionable Propertian tunic of coarse silk' (J. J. Espey: 'Ezra Pound's Mauberley.')

35. *pianola*: mechanism for automatic piano-playing. A modern equivalent would be juke-box. Some 'replacement' for the work of a great classical poetess!

37. Christ, the non-artistic, purely moral figure, has super-seded Dionysus, the god of song, passion, and ecstasy.

38–9. 'The rich pagan ceremonials and god-feasts had to give way to feeble gutless Christian worship.'

40. In Shakespeare's *Tempest* Caliban is a bestial servant, Ariel a spirit.

41–4. The philosopher Heraclitus taught that everything was in a state of flux ('flowing')—nothing could last. But this 'tawdry cheapness' looks horribly lasting.

46. *after Samothrace*: perhaps a reference to the Turkish overrunning of Samothrace and massacring of the population.

47–8. 'The Beautiful is judged purely by its money value in the market place.' (Espey).

49–52. *Faun*: a Roman animal-god. *wafer*: the 'bread' of the Christian Communion service. *circumcision*: the symbolic mark of Jewish faith. The great superstitions, rituals, and symbols are gone; instead we have the Press and the vote. Again, some replacement!

55–6. Pound's bitter dismissal of democracy. By modern electoral processes we are liable to elect a scoundrel or half-man to rule us where before there was a tyrant (*Pisistratus*).

57–60. Apollo was the god of light, music, prophecy; miser-ably the poet asks 'who is there to celebrate today?' Line 58 is translated in line 59.

IV and V. The First World War raised the question of what people were dying *for*. (At this stage the soldiers were, officially, volunteers.) Some did fight in belief that the fight was right, and some sincerely fought *pro domo* (for home) and *pro patria* (for native-land). The motives of others were very mixed, Pound shrewdly but not harshly observes.

72–4. Compare Wilfred Owen's poem on page 118, for a striking coincidence of phrase and idea.

89. Among the myriad who died were some of the best kind of people.

94–5. Pound's view of our cultural inheritance is not, of course, this. But he sees that this is all the significance which that inheritance had for most of those who died: and his poem is a lament both for these and for the 'botched' civilization they came from.

CANTO XVII

All Pound's CANTOS are difficult reading, and one must not look in them for logical neatly-linked ideas. CANTO XVII has been chosen for this book because, although a 'meaning' cannot be easily found within it, there is plenty one can recognize and appreciate in the descriptions—their clarity and brilliance—and in the beautifully-weighted, delicate verse-movement (the arrangement of the lines on the page is a guide to their speaking).

CANTO XVII creates a Mediterranean landscape; from the first words it is more than a *painting*, for the senses of touch and smell and hearing are immediately enlisted. Greece seems at first the likely setting—'the cities set in their hills', and the gods lightly treading the vivid landscape. But *palazzi* (line 17) indicates Italy, and the man who comes in a boat speaks of a city like Venice, where the marble forms 'arbours of stone' and where the silver beaks of gondolas rise and cross. The names *Borso*, *Carmagnola*, and *Sigismundo* are those of Italian Renaissance noblemen. Crudely, then, one may say that Pound in this poem is re-creating for us some of the wonder of the classical Mediterranean lands. The vitality and divinity so keenly missed in the modern world of MAUBERLEY are breathtakingly brought before us here. CANTO XVII in fact acts as a vision of an Elysian place, a Heaven on earth, after several earlier Hell-like Cantos.

The notes on names, below, may help a little; but of course they do not begin to explain the poem. There are other references and names in the poem which I have not been able to find explanations of; some of them may have been simply invented by Pound.

6. IO ZAGREUS: 'O Dionysus!' (He was the god of wine, fertility, and ecstasy.)

20. *Chrysophrase* is an apple-green kind of chalcedony (quartz-type stone).

24. Nereus was a Neptune-like figure in Homer, and the sea-maidens the Nereids were his daughters. *Nerea* seems to be an imagined mermaid-like figure.

41. *malachite*: green coppery mineral taking high polish.

47. *Hermes* (Mercury) was the messenger-god; *Athene* the goddess of wisdom.

73. *i vitrei*: the glass-makers. Pound is referring to the highly-developed civilization of Renaissance Venice, whose achievements he admires though he finds corruption there ('the men of craft' may be ambiguous).

89. *sistrum*: an Egyptian metal rattle.

97. Seems to be an adapted quote from the *Odyssey* (where *Circe* is a beautiful witch).

T. S. Eliot

T. S. Eliot was born in St. Louis, Missouri in 1888. After a Harvard degree he came to Europe to complete his studies and, because of the war, stayed in England, where he did low-paid work as a teacher and bank-clerk, while writing reviews of startling originality. Like many other young artists, he was helped and influenced at this time by Ezra Pound, on whose advice he is said to have cut his most famous poem, THE WASTE LAND (1922), by about half. In his youth Eliot was understandably regarded as a rebel, because his new ideas were radical; but he was always of a sober (indeed shy) nature, and with his conversion to Anglo-Catholicism in 1927 and his Professorship of Poetry at Harvard in 1932 he became a highly respectable and respected figure, giving talks on religion and culture and, as a director of Faber and Faber, doing much to help young poets. In his later years he wrote less poetry but a number of verse plays. He died in 1965.

When Eliot began publishing poetry Victorian Romanticism was at its last gasp, in the chatty, matter-of-fact, but basically sentimental poems of the 'Georgians', of whom Rupert Brooke was the most popular. Eliot, both by personal inclination and for what he sensed to be the needs of the time, reacted sharply against nineteenth-century English poetry and its criticism. In his own reviewing he asserted the excellence of half-forgotten sixteenth- and seventeenth-century writers, and in his poetry made brainwork and a sense of Wit again important. Irony is probably the most pervasive characteristic of his early London poems: not only the ironic wit of the seventeenth-century Metaphysicals, but also a modern impudent, allusive irony derived from the French symbolist Jules Laforgue and from Ezra Pound.

Later Eliot's poetry becomes more earnest and broadly

philosophical, though THE WASTE LAND, certainly a philosophical comment on twentieth-century society, is still wickedly infested with literary sick jokes and embellished with exaggeratedly learned notes. The spirit of THE WASTE LAND seems pessimistic, but its message is one of exhortation to better things, and *Ash Wednesday* (1930) and *Four Quartets* (1944) are poems firmly based in Christian faith, though always of a sombre kind. (Eliot is never exuberant.) *Four Quartets*, arguably Eliot's finest work, is easier to understand than the earlier poems: the literary allusions have almost disappeared and there is no deliberate cultivation of obscurity.

Eliot is undeniably a difficult poet, and the more irritating for this because the difficulty is often quite deliberate. But he is not inaccessible; and he would himself have considered that he had failed if his poems did not communicate a great part of their meaning to an intelligent reader unfurnished with notes and commentaries. It is important not to *make* difficulties for ourselves, particularly in early readings of poetry; the clever critics should be left alone, at least for a while. Take things at their face value, and don't try to do too much allegorical interpreting. The second paragraph of EAST COKER, for example, is about a lane leading into a village, on a hot afternoon; and suggestions that the lane is life and the village one's destiny seem to me grotesque and crude. Eliot knew what he was doing better than that; when he wants to be allegorical he gives clear sign-posts (and avoids descriptions of this concrete immediacy).

Above all, Eliot is accessible (like many great poets) through his verse. Some of us were brought up on his *Practical Cat* poems, or a little later, perhaps, on *Sweeney Agonistes*, in which conventional popular verse-forms are handled with the utmost skill. PRUFROCK is haunting and disturbing in its incantations (listen if possible to Eliot's reading of it on record); the epigrams of WHISPERS OF IMMORTALITY have become popular quotations. Throughout his work the craftsmanship and lucidity of the verse compel us to close attention, and can be a guide to our understanding.

The Love-Song of J. Alfred Prufrock

S'io credesse che mia risposta fosse
A persona che mai tornasse al mondo,
Questa fiamma staria senza piu scosse.
Ma perciocche giammai di questo fondo
Non torno vivo alcun, s'i'odo il vero,
Senza tema d'infamia ti rispondo.

Let us go then, you and I,
When the evening is spread out against the sky
Like a patient etherised upon a table;
Let us go, through certain half-deserted streets,
The muttering retreats
Of restless nights in one-night cheap hotels
And sawdust restaurants with oyster-shells:
Streets that follow like a tedious argument
Of insidious intent
To lead you to an overwhelming question . . .
Oh, do not ask, 'What is it?'
Let us go and make our visit.

In the room the women come and go
Talking of Michelangelo.

The yellow fog that rubs its back upon the window-panes
The yellow smoke that rubs its muzzle on the window-
       panes
Licked its tongue into the corners of the evening,
Lingered upon the pools that stand in drains,
Let fall upon its back the soot that falls from chimneys,
Slipped by the terrace, made a sudden leap,
And seeing that it was a soft October night,
Curled once about the house, and fell asleep.

And indeed there will be time
For the yellow smoke that slides along the street
Rubbing its back upon the window-panes;
There will be time, there will be time
To prepare a face to meet the faces that you meet;
There will be time to murder and create,
And time for all the works and days of hands
That lift and drop a question on your plate;
Time for you and time for me,
And time yet for a hundred indecisions,
And for a hundred visions and revisions,
Before the taking of a toast and tea.

In the room the women come and go
Talking of Michelangelo.

And indeed there will be time
To wonder, 'Do I dare?' and, 'Do I dare?'
Time to turn back and descend the stair,
With a bald spot in the middle of my hair—
(They will say: 'How his hair is growing thin!')
My morning coat, my collar mounting firmly to the chin,
My necktie rich and modest, but asserted by a simple
          pin—
(They will say: 'But how his arms and legs are thin!')
Do I dare
Disturb the universe?
In a minute there is time
For decisions and revisions which a minute will reverse.

For I have known them all already, known them all—
Have known the evenings, mornings, afternoons,
I have measured out my life with coffee-spoons;
I know the voices dying with a dying fall

Beneath the music from a farther room.
　　So how should I presume?

And I have known the eyes already, known them all—
The eyes that fix you in a formulated phrase,
And when I am formulated, sprawling on a pin,
When I am pinned and wriggling on the wall,
Then how should I begin
To spit out all the butt-ends of my days and ways?
　　And how should I presume?

And I have known the arms already, known them all—
Arms that are braceleted and white and bare
(But in the lamplight, downed with light brown hair!)
Is it a perfume from a dress
That makes me so digress?
Arms that lie along a table, or wrap about a shawl.
　　And should I then presume?
　　And how should I begin?

Shall I say, I have gone at dusk through narrow streets
And watched the smoke that rises from the pipes
Of lonely men in shirt-sleeves, leaning out of
　　　　　　windows? . . .

I should have been a pair of ragged claws
Scuttling across the floors of silent seas.

And the afternoon, the evening, sleeps so peacefully!
Smoothed by long fingers,
Asleep . . . tired . . . or it malingers,
Stretched on the floor, here beside you and me.

Should I, after tea and cakes and ices,
Have the strength to force the moment to its crisis?
But though I have wept and fasted, wept and prayed,
Though I have seen my head (grown slightly bald)
           brought in upon a platter,
I am no prophet—and here's no great matter;
I have seen the moment of my greatness flicker,
And I have seen the eternal Footman hold my coat, and
           snicker,
And in short, I was afraid.

And would it have been worth it, after all,
After the cups, the marmalade, the tea,
Among the porcelain, among some talk of you and me,
Would it have been worth while,
To have bitten off the matter with a smile,
To have squeezed the universe into a ball
To roll it toward some overwhelming question,
To say: 'I am Lazarus, come from the dead,
Come back to tell you all, I shall tell you all'—
If one, settling a pillow by her head,
      Should say: 'That is not what I meant at all.
      That is not it, at all.'

And would it have been worth it, after all,
Would it have been worth while,
After the sunsets and the dooryards and the sprinkled
           streets,
After the novels, after the teacups, after the skirts that
           trail along the floor—
And this, and so much more?—
It is impossible to say just what I mean!
But as if a magic lantern threw the nerves in patterns on
           a screen:

Would it have been worth while
If one, settling a pillow or throwing off a shawl,
And turning toward the window should say:
    'That is not it at all,
     That is not what I meant, at all.'

No! I am not Prince Hamlet, nor was meant to be;
Am an attendant lord, one that will do
To swell a progress, start a scene or two,
Advise the prince; no doubt, an easy tool,
Deferential, glad to be of use,
Politic, cautious, and meticulous;
Full of high sentence, but a bit obtuse;
At times, indeed, almost ridiculous—
Almost, at times, the Fool.

I grow old . . . I grow old . . .
I shall wear the bottoms of my trousers rolled.

Shall I part my hair behind? Do I dare to eat a peach?
I shall wear white flannel trousers, and walk upon the
       beach.
I have heard the mermaids singing, each to each.

I do not think that they will sing to me.

I have seen them riding seaward on the waves
Combing the white hair of the waves blown back
When the wind blows the water white and black.

We have lingered in the chambers of the sea
By sea-girls wreathed with seaweed red and brown
Till human voices wake us, and we drown.

The Hippopotamus

*And when this epistle is read among you, cause it
that be read also in the church of the Laodiceans.*

The broad-backed hippopotamus
Rests on his belly in the mud;
Although he seems so firm to us
He is merely flesh and blood.

Flesh and blood is weak and frail,
Susceptible to nervous shock;
While the True Church can never fail
For it is based upon a rock.

The hippo's feeble steps may err
In compassing material ends,
While the True Church need never stir
To gather in its dividends.

The 'potamus can never reach
The mango on the mango-tree;
But fruits of pomegranate and peach
Refresh the Church from over sea.

At mating time the hippo's voice
Betrays inflexions hoarse and odd,
But every week we hear rejoice
The Church, at being one with God.

The hippopotamus's day
Is passed in sleep; at night he hunts;
God works in a mysterious way—
The Church can sleep and feed at once.

70

I saw the 'potamus take wing
Ascending from the damp savannas,
And quiring angels round him sing
The praise of God, in loud hosannas.

Blood of the Lamb shall wash him clean
And him shall heavenly arms enfold,
Among the saints he shall be seen
Performing on a harp of gold.

He shall be washed as white as snow,
By all the martyr'd virgins kist,
While the True Church remains below
Wrapt in the old miasmal mist.

Whispers of Immortality

Webster was much possessed by death
And saw the skull beneath the skin;
And breastless creatures under ground
Leaned backward with a lipless grin.

Daffodil bulbs instead of balls
Stared from the sockets of the eyes!
He knew that thought clings round dead limbs
Tightening its lusts and luxuries.

Donne, I suppose, was such another
Who found no substitute for sense,
To seize and clutch and penetrate;
Expert beyond experience,

He knew the anguish of the marrow
The ague of the skeleton;
No contact possible to flesh
Allayed the fever of the bone.

Grishkin is nice: her Russian eye
Is underlined for emphasis;
Uncorseted, her friendly bust
Gives promise of pneumatic bliss.

The couched Brazilian jaguar
Compels the scampering marmoset
With subtle effluence of cat;
Grishkin has a maisonette;

The sleek Brazilian jaguar
Does not in its arboreal gloom
Distil so rank a feline smell
As Grishkin in a drawing-room.

And even the Abstract Entities
Circumambulate her charm;
But our lot crawls between dry ribs
To keep our metaphysics warm.

from *The Waste Land*
What the Thunder Said

After the torchlight red on sweaty faces
After the frosty silence in the gardens
After the agony in stony places
The shouting and the crying
325 Prison and palace and reverberation
Of thunder of spring over distant mountains
He who was living is now dead
We who were living are now dying
With a little patience

330 Here is no water but only rock
Rock and no water and the sandy road
The road winding above among the mountains
Which are mountains of rock without water
If there were water we should stop and drink
335 Amongst the rock one cannot stop or think
Sweat is dry and feet are in the sand
If there were only water amongst the rock
Dead mountain mouth of carious teeth that cannot
      spit
Here one can neither stand nor lie nor sit
340 There is not even silence in the mountains
But dry sterile thunder without rain
There is not even solitude in the mountains
But red sullen faces sneer and snarl
From doors of mudcracked houses
345   If there were water
      And no rock
      If there were rock
      And also water

74

And water
A spring   350
A pool among the rock
If there were the sound of water only
Not the cicada
And dry grass singing
But sound of water over a rock   355
Where the hermit-thrush sings in the pine trees
Drip drop drip drop drop drop drop
But there is no water

Who is the third who walks always beside you?
When I count, there are only you and I together   360
But when I look ahead up the white road
There is always another one walking beside you
Gliding wrapt in a brown mantle, hooded
I do not know whether a man or a woman
—But who is that on the other side of you?   365

What is that sound high in the air
Murmur of maternal lamentation
Who are those hooded hordes swarming
Over endless plains, stumbling in cracked earth
Ringed by the flat horizon only   370
What is the city over the mountains
Cracks and reforms and bursts in the violet air
Falling towers
Jerusalem Athens Alexandria
Vienna London   375
Unreal
A woman drew her long black hair out tight
And fiddled whisper music on those strings
And bats with baby faces in the violet light
Whistled, and beat their wings   380

And crawled head downward down a blackened wall
And upside down in air were towers
Tolling reminiscent bells, that kept the hours
And voices singing out of empty cisterns and
    exhausted wells.

385 In this decayed home among the mountains
In the faint moonlight, the grass is singing
Over the tumbled graves, about the chapel
There is the empty chapel, only the wind's home.
It has no windows, and the door swings,
390 Dry bones can harm no one.
Only a cock stood on the rooftree
Co co rico co co rico
In a flash of lightning. Then a damp gust
Bringing rain

395 Ganga was sunken, and the limp leaves
Waited for rain, while the black clouds
Gathered far distant, over Himavant.
The jungle crouched, humped in silence.
Then spoke the thunder
400 DA
Datta: what have we given?
My friend, blood shaking my heart
The awful daring of a moment's surrender
Which an age of prudence can never retract
405 By this, and this only, we have existed
Which is not to be found in our obituaries
Or in memories draped by the beneficent spider
Or under seals broken by the lean solicitor
In our empty rooms
410 DA
Dayadhvam: I have heard the key

Turn in the door once and once only
We think of the key, each in his prison
Thinking of the key, each confirms a prison
Only at nightfall, aethereal rumours   415
Revive for a moment a broken Coriolanus
DA
Damyata: The boat responded
Gaily, to the hand expert with sail and oar
The sea was calm, your heart would have responded 420
Gaily, when invited, beating obedient
To controlling hands

                            I sat upon the shore
Fishing, with the arid plain behind me.
Shall I at least set my lands in order?   425
London Bridge is falling down falling down falling
        down
Poi s'ascose nel foco che gli affina
Quando fiam uti chelidon—O swallow swallow
Le Prince d'Aquitaine a la tour abolie
These fragments I have shored against my ruins   430
Why then Ile fit you. Hieronymo's mad againe.
Datta. Dayadhvam. Damyata.
                Shantih shantih shantih

The Hollow Men

A penny for the Old Guy

I

We are the hollow men
We are the stuffed men
Leaning together
Headpiece filled with straw. Alas!
Our dried voices, when
We whisper together
Are quiet and meaningless
As wind in dry grass
Or rats' feet over broken glass
In our dry cellar

Shape without form, shade without colour,
Paralysed force, gesture without motion;

Those who have crossed
With direct eyes, to death's other Kingdom
Remember us—if at all—not as lost
Violent souls, but only
As the hollow men
The stuffed men.

II

Eyes I dare not meet in dreams
In death's dream kingdom
These do not appear:
There, the eyes are
Sunlight on a broken column
There, is a tree swinging

And voices are   25
In the wind's singing
More distant and more solemn
Than a fading star.

Let me be no nearer
In death's dream kingdom   30
Let me also wear
Such deliberate disguises
Rat's coat, crowskin, crossed staves
In a field
Behaving as the wind behaves   35
No nearer—

Not that final meeting
In the twilight kingdom

III

This is the dead land
This is cactus land   40
Here the stone images
Are raised, here they receive
The supplication of a dead man's hand
Under the twinkle of a fading star.

Is it like this   45
In death's other kingdom
Waking alone
At the hour when we are
Trembling with tenderness
Lips that would kiss   50
Form prayers to broken stone.

The eyes are not here
There are no eyes here
In this valley of dying stars
55　In this hollow valley
This broken jaw of our lost kingdoms

In this last of meeting places
We grope together
And avoid speech
60　Gathered on this beach of the tumid river

Sightless, unless
The eyes reappear
As the perpetual star
Multifoliate rose
65　Of death's twilight kingdom
The hope only
Of empty men.

V

Here we go round the prickly pear
Prickly pear prickly pear
70　*Here we go round the prickly pear*
At five o'clock in the morning.

Between the idea
And the reality
Between the motion
75　And the act
Falls the Shadow
　　　　　　　For Thine is the Kingdom

Between the conception
And the creation
Between the emotion
And the response   80
Falls the Shadow
                              Life is very long

Between the desire
And the spasm   85
Between the potency
And the existence
Between the essence
And the descent
Falls the Shadow   90
                    For Thine is the Kingdom

For Thine is
Life is
For Thine is the

This is the way the world ends   95
This is the way the world ends
This is the way the world ends
Not with a bang but a whimper.

Journey of the Magi

'A cold coming we had of it,
Just the worst time of the year
For a journey, and such a long journey:
The ways deep and the weather sharp,
The very dead of winter.'
And the camels galled, sore-footed, refractory,
Lying down in the melting snow.
There were times we regretted
The summer palaces on slopes, the terraces,
And the silken girls bringing sherbet.
Then the camel men cursing and grumbling
And running away, and wanting their liquor and women,
And the night-fires going out, and the lack of shelters,
And the cities hostile and the towns unfriendly
And the villages dirty and charging high prices:
A hard time we had of it.
At the end we preferred to travel all night,
Sleeping in snatches,
With the voices singing in our ears, saying
That this was all folly.

Then at dawn we came down to a temperate valley,
Wet, below the snow line, smelling of vegetation;
With a running stream and a water-mill beating the
        darkness,
And three trees on the low sky,
And an old white horse galloped away in the meadow.
Then we came to a tavern with vine-leaves over the
        lintel,
Six hands at an open door dicing for pieces of silver,
And feet kicking the empty wine-skins.

But there was no information, and so we continued
And arrived at evening, not a moment too soon
Finding the place; it was (you may say) satisfactory.

All this was a long time ago, I remember,
And I would do it again, but set down
This set down
This: were we led all that way for
Birth or Death? There was a Birth, certainly,
We had evidence and no doubt. I had seen birth and
        death,
But had thought they were different; this Birth was
Hard and bitter agony for us, like Death, our death.
We returned to our places, these Kingdoms,
But no longer at ease here, in the old dispensation,
With an alien people clutching their gods.
I should be glad of another death.

East Coker

I

In my beginning is my end. In succession
Houses rise and fall, crumble, are extended,
Are removed, destroyed, restored, or in their place
Is an open field, or a factory, or a by-pass.
5   Old stone to new building, old timber to new fires,
Old fires to ashes, and ashes to the earth
Which is already flesh, fur, and faeces,
Bone of man and beast, cornstalk and leaf.
Houses live and die: there is a time for building
10   And a time for living and for generation
And a time for the wind to break the loosened pane
And to shake the wainscot where the field-mouse trots
And to shake the tattered arras woven with a silent motto.

In my beginning is my end. Now the light falls
15   Across the open field, leaving the deep lane
Shuttered with branches, dark in the afternoon,
Where you lean against a bank while a van passes,
And the deep lane insists on the direction
Into the village, in the electric heat
20   Hypnotized. In a warm haze the sultry light
Is absorbed, not refracted, by grey stone.
The dahlias sleep in the empty silence.
Wait for the early owl.

                In that open field
If you do not come too close, if you do not come too
25   close,
On a summer midnight, you can hear the music
Of the weak pipe and the little drum
And see them dancing around the bonfire

The association of man and woman
In daunsinge, signifying matrimonie—   30
A dignified and commodious sacrament.
Two and two, necessarye coniunction,
Holding eche other by the hand or arm
Whiche betokeneth concorde. Round and round the fire
Leaping through the flames, or joined in circles,   35
Rustically solemn or in rustic laughter
Lifting heavy feet in clumsy shoes,
Earth feet, loam feet, lifted in country mirth
Mirth of those long since under earth
Nourishing the corn. Keeping time,   40
Keeping the rhythm in their dancing
As in their living in the living seasons
The time of the seasons and the constellations
The time of milking and the time of harvest
The time of the coupling of man and woman   45
And that of beasts. Feet rising and falling.
Eating and drinking. Dung and death.

Dawn points, and another day
Prepares for heat and silence. Out at sea the dawn wind
Wrinkles and slides. I am here   50
Or there, or elsewhere. In my beginning.

II

What is the late November doing
With the disturbance of the spring
And creatures of the summer heat
And snowdrops writhing under feet   55
And hollyhocks that aim too high
Red into grey and tumble down
Late roses filled with early snow?

Thunder rolled by the rolling stars
60 Simulates triumphal cars
Deployed in constellated wars
Scorpion fights against the Sun
Until the Sun and Moon go down
Comets weep and Leonids fly
65 Hunt the heavens and the plains
Whirled in a vortex that shall bring
The world to that destructive fire
Which burns before the ice-cap reigns.

That was a way of putting it—not very satisfactory:
70 A periphrastic study in a worn-out poetical fashion,
Leaving one still with the intolerable wrestle
With words and meanings. The poetry does not matter
It was not (to start again) what one had expected.
What was to be the value of the long looked forward to,
75 Long hoped for calm, the autumnal serenity
And the wisdom of age? Had they deceived us
Or deceived themselves, the quiet-voiced elders,
Bequeathing us merely a receipt for deceit?
The serenity only a deliberate hebetude,
80 The wisdom only the knowledge of dead secrets
Useless in the darkness into which they peered
Or from which they turned their eyes. There is, it seems
        to us,
At best, only a limited value
In the knowledge derived from experience.
85 The knowledge imposes a pattern, and falsifies,
For the pattern is new in every moment
And every moment is a new and shocking
Valuation of all we have been. We are only undeceived
Of that which, deceiving, could no longer harm.
90 In the middle, not only in the middle of the way

But all the way, in a dark wood, in a bramble,
On the edge of a grimpen, where is no secure foothold,
And menaced by monsters, fancy lights,
Risking enchantment. Do not let me hear
Of the wisdom of old men, but rather of their folly,   95
Their fear of fear and frenzy, their fear of possession,
Of belonging to another, or to others, or to God.
The only wisdom we can hope to acquire
Is the wisdom of humility: humility is endless.

The houses are all gone under the sea.   100

The dancers are all gone under the hill.

III

O dark dark dark. They all go into the dark,
The vacant interstellar spaces, the vacant into the vacant,
The captains, merchant bankers, eminent men of letters,
The generous patrons of art, the statesmen and the
        rulers,   105
Distinguished civil servants, chairmen of many
        committees,
Industrial lords and petty contractors, all go into the
        dark,
And dark the Sun and Moon, and the Almanach de
        Gotha
And the Stock Exchange Gazette, the Directory of
        Directors,
And cold the sense and lost the motive of action.   110
And we all go with them, into the silent funeral,
Nobody's funeral, for there is no one to bury.
I said to my soul, be still, and let the dark come upon you
Which shall be the darkness of God. As, in a theatre,

115 The lights are extinguished, for the scene to be changed
With a hollow rumble of wings, with a movement of
       darkness on darkness,
And we know that the hills and the trees, the distant
       panorama
And the bold imposing façade are all being rolled away—
Or as, when an underground train, in the tube, stops too
       long between stations
120 And the conversation rises and slowly fades into silence
And you see behind every face the mental emptiness
       deepen
Leaving only the growing terror of nothing to think
       about;
Or when, under ether, the mind is conscious but
       conscious of nothing—
I said to my soul, be still, and wait without hope
125 For hope would be hope for the wrong thing; wait
       without love
For love would be love of the wrong thing; there is yet
       faith
But the faith and the love and the hope are all in the
       waiting.
Wait without thought, for you are not yet ready for
       thought:
So the darkness shall be the light, and the stillness the
       dancing.
130 Whisper of running streams, and winter lightning.
The wild thyme unseen and the wild strawberry,
The laughter in the garden, echoed ecstasy
Not lost, but requiring, pointing to the agony
Of death and birth.

135   You say I am repeating
Something I have said before. I shall say it again.

Shall I say it again? In order to arrive there,
To arrive where you are, to get from where you are not,
    You must go by a way wherein there is no ecstasy.
In order to arrive at what you do not know   140
    You must go by a way which is the way of ignorance.
In order to possess what you do not possess
    You must go by the way of dispossession.
In order to arrive at what you are not
    You must go through the way in which you are not.   145
And what you do not know is the only thing you know
And what you own is what you do not own
And where you are is where you are not.

IV

The wounded surgeon plies the steel
That questions the distempered part;   150
Beneath the bleeding hands we feel
The sharp compassion of the healer's art
Resolving the enigma of the fever chart.

Our only health is the disease
If we obey the dying nurse   155
Whose constant care is not to please
But to remind of our, and Adam's curse,
And that, to be restored, our sickness must grow worse.

The whole earth is our hospital
Endowed by the ruined millionaire,   160
Wherein, if we do well, we shall
Die of the absolute paternal care
That will not leave us, but prevents us everywhere.

The chill ascends from feet to knees,
The fever sings in mental wires.   165

If to be warmed, then I must freeze
And quake in frigid purgatorial fires
Of which the flame is roses, and the smoke is briars.

170 The dripping blood our only drink,
The bloody flesh our only food:
In spite of which we like to think
That we are sound, substantial flesh and blood—
Again, in spite of that, we call this Friday good.

V

So here I am, in the middle way, having had twenty
      years—
Twenty years largely wasted, the years of *l'entre deux*
175   *guerres*—
Trying to learn to use words, and every attempt
Is a wholly new start, and a different kind of failure
Because one has only learnt to get the better of words
For the thing one no longer has to say, or the way in
      which
180 One is no longer disposed to say it. And so each venture
Is a new beginning, a raid on the inarticulate
With shabby equipment always deteriorating
In the general mess of imprecision of feeling,
Undisciplined squads of emotion. And what there is to
      conquer
185 By strength and submission, has already been discovered
Once or twice, or several times, by men whom one
      cannot hope
To emulate—but there is no competition—
There is only the fight to recover what has been lost
And found and lost again and again: and now, under
      conditions

That seem unpropitious. But perhaps neither gain nor
      loss.   190
For us, there is only the trying. The rest is not our
      business.

Home is where one starts from. As we grow older
The world becomes stranger, the pattern more
      complicated
Of dead and living. Not the intense moment
Isolated, with no before and after,   195
But a lifetime burning in every moment
And not the lifetime of one man only
But of old stones that cannot be deciphered.
There is a time for the evening under starlight,
A time for the evening under lamplight   200
(The evening with the photograph album).
Love is most nearly itself
When here and now cease to matter.
Old men ought to be explorers
Here and there does not matter   205
We must be still and still moving
Into another intensity
For a further union, a deeper communion
Through the dark cold and the empty desolation,
The wave cry, the wind cry, the vast waters   210
Of the petrel and the porpoise. In my end is my
      beginning.

Notes

I have drawn several times here from George Williamson's *A Reader's Guide to T. S. Eliot*

THE LOVE-SONG OF J. ALFRED PRUFROCK
Epigraph, from Dante's *Inferno*:

'If I thought that my reply were addressed to one who could ever return to the world, this flame should shake no more; but since none ever did return alive from this depth (if what I hear be true), without fear of infamy I answer you.'

In some ways this poem is a disclosure, Prufrock laying himself unusually open.

Note the absurd primness of the main character's name: what a person to be singing a love-song! In fact, it is, we discover, a sort of non-love-song: this is a poem of twentieth-century defeat and impotence, told—in modern manner—in a self-mocking tone. Prufrock is on his way to a drawing-room, to make his amorous proposal: but he shrinks from the whole business; he lacks the bravado and heroism. And indeed he never makes his proposal: the second half of the poem is an acceptance of defeat.

The mood of the poem is opposed to all Romantic traditions. The evening, in line 3, is passionless: the fog of London is an unheroic setting, and in its cat-role it curls up and goes to sleep; 'there will be time' for 'a hundred indecisions . . . visions and revisions' (delicious word-play!). The heroic figure of Michelangelo looms up in the drawing-room conversation only by way of contrast. . . . 'Do I dare?' The drawing-room itself is immensely wearying and (to this little man 'pinned and wriggling on the wall') terrifying.

Briefly Prufrock tries to prepare a speech; 'Shall I say . . .' —but he gives up the whole idea in the despairing grimace:

'I should have been a pair of ragged claws/Scuttling across the floors of silent seas'—in other words, he wishes he had never been born, wishes he were dead, wishes the earth would swallow him up.

No, he would never have been capable of it, in spite of all his plans, his summoning-up of courage. She might have said No in amazement and accused him of misinterpreting her kindness—'That is not what I meant at all'—and for the self-conscious Prufrock such a moment would be agonizing (the terrible image of the nerves in the magic lantern). 'Squeezed the universe into a ball to roll it . . .' is an ironic reference to the passionate cavalier lover in Andrew Marvell's *To His Coy Mistress* ('Let us roll all our strength and all/Our sweetness up into one ball'). By referring to Lazarus Prufrock perhaps means that his secret feelings have been buried for a time, and would now be revealed.

In the last section Prufrock concludes that he is not a heroic figure such as Hamlet (Hamlet of all tragic heroes is the one noted for postponing his heroic deeds—'There will be time to murder'; Prufrock has nothing else in common with him). His admission of his inadequacy is gradual, grudging, embarrassing to us. His boldest gestures will be to wear his trousers in the new fashion, to change his hair-style to hide his baldness, and so on. He will walk on the beach, but no mermaids will sing to him. Yet he has long dreamt of mermaids in escapist Romantic visions, so much so that he is unfitted for real life (compare James Thurber's Walter Mitty or Shakespeare's Richard II).

THE HIPPOPOTAMUS
The epigraph is a satiric lifting of some closing words in the Epistle to the Colossians. Critics have pursued the reference to the Laodiceans diligently, but the satiric point seems obvious and simple to me: read this poem as if it were a solemn epistle, and have it circulated among the churches.

The poem itself needs no comment. Eliot was at this time, one need hardly say, not a Christian.

One of the most famous Romantic poems is Wordsworth's *Ode on Intimations of Immortality from Recollections of Early Childhood*. Webster and Donne were Jacobean writers, obsessed with death; this made them plunge into the physical life greedily, and that in turn gave them a vigorous, vital sense of abstract questions. That is, by much contact with flesh, Donne knew that no physical indulgence, no 'contact possible to flesh', could soothe the fear of death and its aftermath. Twentieth-century mankind, however, is obsessed with the physically attractive Grishkin (even the abstract truths for which Donne and Webster groped walk round her, enslaved), but—last two lines—we shy off really doing something about it, we turn back to dry theorizing to make our metaphysical speculations (which, it is implied, we thereby weaken).

The ideas, then, are perhaps excessively contorted and compressed. But the skill of the verse, the wit and epigrammatic power, make this still a memorable poem.

WHAT THE THUNDER SAID

Eliot published notes with THE WASTE LAND and more or less instructed his readers to do a lot of hard work. But his method is not a mere perversity. As with the French symbolists of the nineteenth century, this indirect, perplexing communication is saying complex, ambiguous things which could not be completely paraphrased but which do come through. WHAT THE THUNDER SAID is the last section; the earlier passages have presented images of superstition, primitive rituals and myths, and the materialist poverty and ugliness of twentieth-century life (repeatedly contrasted, by literary ironies, to the rich and graceful past). The poem, then, seems to be questioning man's purpose and position in the world: the city life that has 'out-grown' primitive superstition seems so dead that perhaps we should take another look at the superstitions themselves.

The poet's notes tell us that, 'In the first part of Part V three themes are employed: the journey to Emmaus, the approach to the Chapel Perilous . . ., and the present decay of eastern Europe.'

The journey to Emmaus was the journey of disciples some weeks after Christ's death who suddenly discovered Christ walking beside them. This idea of some hope is contradicted, however, by the images of desert and of civilization destroyed. These are the main themes of lines 322–94. The first paragraph seems to relate mainly to Christ's death. (The tone of 329–30 is similar to that of the last line of JOURNEY OF THE MAGI.) The next two paragraphs present the desert, the Waste Land, the claustrophobic repetitions suggesting exhaustion and thirst, especially in the agonizing longing of lines 346–58. There is no difficulty here. The paragraph beginning at 359 clearly describes the journey to Emmaus, but is linked by Eliot's note to Antarctic explorers, on the point of exhaustion, who had a similar sense that there was always with them one more person than had been counted. The next paragraph describes civilization in collapse, and finally in complete decay. There are a number of references to earlier sections of the poem. By a gentle transition ('empty cisterns', 'exhausted wells', 'decayed hole') we move to the Chapel Perilous of chivalric myth. But it is no longer Perilous—the myths are dead. The cock however seems to announce something; probably it is a weathercock rather than a real one, lit up by lightning and making us think of weather . . . rain. Rain is release from the desert, and since Eliot explicitly says there are references in the poem 'to vegetation ceremonies' it has some sacred significance. Rivers are sacred, especially in India, where the poem now moves. 'Datta dayadhavan damyata,' Eliot's note tells us, means, 'Give, sympathize, control.' The lines which follow each order would more or less make this clear anyway.

Give: we have given only in momentary surrender to passion (this was shown earlier in the poem): we have achieved no lasting or profound surrender. We die leaving nothing to

95

show for those moments (whereas if there had been real love its evidence would survive).

Sympathize: but this we fail to do; twentieth-century men are locked in separate cells, and human contact is lacking. (Coriolanus, the proud man, was 'broken' as we are broken by our self-obsession—except in lingering hints at night of the communion there might have been.)

Control: an idealized sea-picture (linking with earlier sections of the poem) of how a proper love can be attained when the heart is under control.

Finally, the poet (understanding what is wrong with the Waste Land, but not himself attaining the Right) is seen preparing for death. He does so by fixing his mind on a few literary fragments:

(i) the disintegration of the modern city (line 426).

(ii) 'Then he hid him in the fire which refines them' (427) —a submission to suffering in order to be purified.

(iii) 'When shall I be as the swallow—O swallow swallow' (line 428)—a wish to have another life or an after-life.

(iv) 'The Prince of Aquitaine at the derelict tower'—suggesting the Chapel Perilous again, but also perhaps the prison of self. The line is from the French symbolist Gérard de Nerval.

The poem ends with a quotation from Kyd's Spanish Tragedy; 'Ile fit you' meaning, more or less, 'this is what I offer you, what is appropriate to you.'

'Shantih', Eliot tells us, is, 'The formal ending to an Upanishad [Sanskrit philosophical treatise]. "The Peace which passeth understanding" is our equivalent to this word.'

THE HOLLOW MEN

Death, in this poem, has two kingdoms: the Hollow Men are in one, waiting to cross to the other. If the first Kingdom (the dream Kingdom) is seen as earthly life, much of the point of the poem lies in the fact that this is nevertheless a kingdom of Death. The mortality and futility of that earthly life seems to be a major theme in the poem. Worse still, both earthly life and after-life are one story of frustration (lines 11–12, 47–51, and the whole of Section V).

There is a pathetic hope in Section IV ('the hope only' means 'merely a hope, nothing more') that the after-life may be a rich flowering and consummation (lines 61–5). But for the rest, there is only cruel mockery—the Guy figures, whispering together their terrible 'Alas!'; the cactus nursery-rhyme; the hope-image of the star 'fading' and 'dying'; and the death of the eyes, dehumanizing.

More general interpretations must be left to individual readers.

JOURNEY OF THE MAGI
The opening of the poem is quoted from Bishop Lancelot Andrewes.

What Biblical images are suggested by 'three trees on the low sky', 'an old white horse', and 'six hands . . . dicing for pieces of silver'?

The last section is the most important. For the wise men, the recognition of the beginning of a new religion and truth is not a time of glory or rejoicing. 'It was (you may say) satis-factory.' They found what they were seeking, but it involved the death of their kingdoms and myths, so that all they had previously lived by became meaningless. Possibly this has a twentieth-century relevance.

EAST COKER
This is the second of four poems published under the title *Four Quartets*. Eliot is by this time a Christian, and the themes of frustration and deprivation have been replaced by an absorption in the mystery of human experience, especially religious experience transcending time. Each Quartet is named after a place important to Eliot's life or ancestors' lives. His family came originally from the village of East Coker, in Somerset. Lines 29–34 are quoted from Sir Thomas Elyot, a Tudor ancestor.

In the Quartets there are comparatively few allusions to material outside the poems, but many allusions to material in the other three poems. Each Quartet is in five sections, and these correspond as will be noted below.

I. This section, in each Quartet, is preoccupied with time, and with moments that seem to cut across time. In this case, we have a statement of the cycle of living and death (compare Ecclesiastes 3), interrupted by a vivid moment on a summer afternoon, when the poet senses the field near him as it was centuries ago, 'on a summer midnight', in a marriage-dance? Note the chiasmus of 'earth . . . mirth . . . mirth . . . earth' in lines 38–9; has it any point?

The last four lines of this section seem like an attempt to collect oneself, after this mystical experience. The French for dawn is *point du jour*: it is the earliest moment of light in the sky.

II. The first half of the second section in each Quartet is a piece of rhetorical poetry ('in a worn-out poetical fashion'). November is disturbed in ways of spring and summer: time has become confused, and anticipates the final bonfire which the world will eventually undergo. The astrology of all this is explained in commentaries on Eliot's poems.

The lines which follow are colloquial, modern, and personal—to do with growing old. Age, Eliot says, is not the wisdom it is normally reckoned to be. One learns how one should have behaved in the past, but the present and future offer new patterns, new problems. Compare lines 178–80 below. One must accept one's lack of wisdom, and be humble. Lines 100–1 seem to refer back to the first section, whose images have now receded (into death? Oblivion, at least).

III. Samson's words, blinded at Gaza, open the section. The dark here seems similar to the Shadow of THE HOLLOW MEN—death, futility, frustration. But at line 113 Eliot introduces us to a different darkness—that of the mystic's surrender of thought and knowledge, his submission of an

98

empty humble soul to God, without preconceptions (lines 124–9). Lines 130–4 echo cryptically images from *Burnt Norton* (the first Quartet): a hint of the kind of revelation God might give? The 'laughter in the garden' was seen in the previous poem as one of those moments which transcended time. Lines 135–48 repeat and develop the ideas of 113–29, but this time in dryer, more abstract paradox. The way to God is the way of negation, of submissive darkness and ignorance. The idea behind this—that intellectual sophistication is a barrier to mystical experience—is common in nineteenth- and twentieth-century literature, and it is interesting to see it appearing in Eliot, who is one of the least Romantic and most rational of modern poets.

IV. Section four is, in all Quartets, a song-like poem, stylized and symbolic. Here it is a poem about Christ's compassion: if we are to be redeemed it will be by his wounds, his blood and flesh (the poem is a Good Friday poem)—but also by purgatorial suffering and death ourselves. Christ is the wounded surgeon, the Church the dying nurse, Adam the ruined millionaire.

V. Section five, in each Quartet, is in two parts: a personal colloquial statement, about writing poetry, and a more lyrical generalized conclusion. The first part here has been much quoted and is clear (it is important, though, to understand exactly what Eliot means, in lines 189–90, by 'under conditions/That seem unpropitious'; for this is an idea which underlies much of his poetry and criticism). The second section sums up much that has been said earlier in the poem, especially in lines 74–99. As an old man, Eliot will still have to explore, seeking in mystical and sombre worlds. The image of sea suggesting infinity, the truth, links with many Romantics as well as with the symbolism of THE WASTE LAND. Finally the opening words of the poem are reversed. An old man, nearing the end of life, is beginning afresh the search for understanding.

Notes like this do not communicate the poem EAST COKER, which should be read again many times without them. In the Quartets Eliot has come far from the young man's cleverness and bitterness: he is no longer afraid of grandeur, music, lyricism, is no longer anxious to assert his own wide reading or his aloofness from emotions mankind has felt through the ages. The Quartets are technically brilliant, but without gimmickry, which can hardly be said of the earlier poems: the humility which the Quartets recommend is an element in their direct and consistent seriousness.

Isaac Rosenberg

Isaac Rosenberg was born in Bristol in 1890, of Jewish parents, and educated at elementary school in London, which he left at 14. He studied art and wrote poetry; in 1914 he went to South Africa for his health, but returned in 1915 to enlist. He was killed in action in 1918.

With poets such as Rosenberg, Wilfred Owen, Sidney Keyes, Alun Lewis, Keith Douglas, it is hard to make an adequate valuation, and it may seem irrelevant and callous to try. They were killed in their twenties, when the talent of most poets is only beginning to mature. The collected works of Isaac Rosenberg, or of Wilfred Owen, contain comparatively few really distinguished poems: most of them, I think, are included in this selection. But the success of these few poems is clear; and their protest against that greatest of slaughters moves us not only by the actual poetry, but by our sense of what might have been.

The precision of Rosenberg's imagery in the war poems, and the assurance of his taut verse lines, are the result of a considerable apprenticeship, as his Collected Poems show. Some elements of late Victorianism survive, such as 'Hark! ... Lo! ... like a girl's dark hair ... or her kisses where a serpent hides' or 'the dark music Blown from Sleep's trumpet'. But far more often in these late poems a strong originality is in control.

Rosenberg never writes in mere documentary complaint, as Owen (effectively) does. Shocked he is; but he is also excited by warfare, in the way men may be excited by bull-fights or sadistic acts; and his finest poetry comes from an appalled struggle to understand and control this sick, nervous energy. Rosenberg's poetry is thus more complex than that of Owen and most war poets, and more disturbing a challenge to our complacency. For one can range oneself satisfactorily with Owen in detestation of warfare, and resolutions to prevent it; but Rosenberg shows us the literal insanity which may take a grip on all of us. DEAD MAN'S DUMP is not so far, it seems to me, from parts of *King Lear* or *Othello*; the truth of the poetry is not the whole truth about mankind, but it is a truth, and it might be *our* 'blood-dazed intelligence beating for light' against 'the tide of the world'.

Marching

(As seen from the left file)

My eyes catch ruddy necks
Sturdily pressed back—
All a red brick moving glint.
Like flaming pendulums, hands
Swing across the khaki—
Mustard-coloured khaki—
To the automatic feet.

We husband the ancient glory
In these bared necks and hands.
Not broke is the forge of Mars;
But a subtler brain beats iron
To shoe the hoofs of death
(Who paws dynamic air now).
Blind fingers loose an iron cloud
To rain immortal darkness
On strong eyes.

The Troop Ship

Grotesque and queerly huddled
Contortionists to twist
The sleepy soul to a sleep,
We lie all sorts of ways
And cannot sleep.
The wet wind is so cold,
And the lurching men so careless,
That, should you drop to a doze,
Winds' fumble or men's feet
Are on your face.

August 1914

What in our lives is burnt
In the fire of this?
The heart's dear granary?
The much we shall miss?

Three lives hath one life—
Iron, honey, gold.
The gold, the honey gone—
Left is the hard and cold.

Iron are our lives
Molten right through our youth.
A burnt space through ripe fields
A fair mouth's broken tooth.

Returning, we hear the larks

Sombre the night is.
And though we have our lives, we know
What sinister threat lurks there.

Dragging these anguished limbs, we only know
This poison-blasted track opens on our camp—
On a little safe sleep.

But hark! joy—joy—strange joy.
Lo! heights of night ringing with unseen larks.
Music showering on our upturned list'ning faces.

Death could drop from the dark
As easily as song—
But song only dropped,
Like a blind man's dreams on the sand
By dangerous tides,
Like a girl's dark hair for she dreams no ruin lies
    there,
Or her kisses where a serpent hides.

Break of Day in the Trenches

The darkness crumbles away—
It is the same old druid Time as ever.
Only a live thing leaps in my hand—
A queer sardonic rat—
As I pull the parapet's poppy
To stick behind my ear.
Droll rat, they would shoot you if they knew
Your cosmopolitan sympathies.
Now you have touched this English hand
You will do the same to a German—
Soon, no doubt, if it be your pleasure
To cross the sleeping green between.
It seems you inwardly grin as you pass
Strong eyes, fine limbs, haughty athletes
Less chanced than you for life,
Bonds to the whims of murder,
Sprawled in the bowels of the earth,
The torn fields of France.
What do you see in our eyes
At the shrieking iron and flame
Hurled through still heavens?
What quaver—what heart aghast?
Poppies whose roots are in man's veins
Drop, and are ever dropping;
But mine in my ear is safe,
Just a little white with the dust.

The Immortals

I killed them, but they would not die.
Yea! all the day and all the night
For them I could not rest nor sleep,
Nor guard from them nor hide in flight.

Then in my agony I turned
And made my hands red in their gore.
In vain—for faster than I slew
They rose more cruel than before.

I killed and killed with slaughter mad;
I killed till all my strength was gone.
And still they rose to torture me,
For Devils only die for fun.

I used to think the Devil hid
In women's smiles and wine's carouse.
I called him Satan, Balzebub,
But now I call him dirty louse.

Louse Hunting

Nudes—stark and glistening,
Yelling in lurid glee. Grinning faces
And raging limbs
Whirl over the floor one fire.
For a shirt verminously busy
Yon soldier tore from his throat, with oaths
Godhead might shrink at, but not the lice.
And soon the shirt was aflare
Over the candle he'd lit while we lay.

Then we all sprang up and stript
To hunt the verminous brood.
Soon like a demons' pantomime
The place was raging.
See the silhouettes agape,
See the gibbering shadows
Mixed with the battled arms on the wall.
See gargantuan hooked fingers
Pluck in supreme flesh
To smutch supreme littleness.
See the merry limbs in hot Highland fling
Because some wizard vermin
Charmed from the quiet this revel
When our ears were half lulled
By the dark music
Blown from Sleep's trumpet.

Dead Man's Dump

The plunging limbers over the shattered track
Racketed with their rusty freight,
Stuck out like many crowns of thorns,
And the rusty stakes like sceptres old
To stay the flood of brutish men
Upon our brothers dear.

The wheels lurched over sprawled dead
But pained them not, though their bones crunched,
Their shut mouths made no moan.
They lie there huddled, friend and foeman,
Man born of man, and born of woman,
And shells go crying over them
From night till night and now.

Earth has waited for them,
All the time of their growth
Fretting for their decay:
Now she has them at last!
In the strength of their strength
Suspended—stopped and held.

What fierce imaginings their dark souls lit?
Earth! have they gone into you!
Somewhere they must have gone,
And flung on your hard back
Is their soul's sack
Emptied of God-ancestralled essences.
Who hurled them out? Who hurled?

None saw their spirits' shadow shake the grass,
Or stood aside for the half used life to pass
Out of those doomed nostrils and the doomed mouth,
When the swift iron burning bee
Drained the wild honey of their youth.

What of us who, flung on the shrieking pyre,
Walk, our usual thoughts untouched,
Our lucky limbs as on ichor fed,
Immortal seeming ever?
Perhaps when the flames beat loud on us,
A fear may choke in our veins
And the startled blood may stop.

The air is loud with death,
The dark air spurts with fire,
The explosions ceaseless are.
Timelessly now, some minutes past,
These dead strode time with vigorous life,
Till the shrapnel called 'An end!'

But not to all. In bleeding pangs
Some borne on stretchers dreamed of home,
Dear things, war-blotted from their hearts.

Maniac Earth! howling and flying, your bowel
Seared by the jagged fire, the iron love,
The impetuous storm of savage love.
Dark Earth! dark Heavens! swinging in chemic
    smoke,
What dead are born when you kiss each soundless
    soul
With lightning and thunder from your mined heart,
Which man's self dug, and his blind fingers loosed?

A man's brains splattered on
A stretcher-bearer's face;
His shook shoulders slipped their load,
But when they bent to look again
The drowning soul was sunk too deep
For human tenderness.

They left this dead with the older dead,
Stretched at the cross roads.

Burnt black by strange decay
Their sinister faces lie,
The lid over each eye,
The grass and coloured clay
More motion have than they,
Joined to the great sunk silences.

Here is one not long dead;
His dark hearing caught our far wheels,
And the choked soul stretched weak hands
To reach the living word the far wheels said,
The blood-dazed intelligence beating for light,
Crying through the suspense of the far torturing
      wheels
Swift for the end to break
Or the wheels to break,
Cried as the tide of the world broke over his sight.

Will they come? Will they ever come?
Even as the mixed hoofs of the mules,
The quivering-bellied mules,
And the rushing wheels all mixed
With his tortured upturned sight.

So we crashed round the bend,
We heard his weak scream,
We heard his very last sound,
And our wheels grazed his dead face.

Notes

MARCHING

What is the point of the repetition of 'khaki' in two lines of the first verse?

This was written before Rosenberg went to the trenches in France. There is a sense of the grandeur of being a soldier, common in poets before they get to the trenches; but also (as there is not in, say, Rupert Brooke) a subtle understanding of the death-force behind military discipline. What words suggest this?

AUGUST 1914

One of the most expressive short poems in English, this—as a bitter charm or motto—seems to say as much as needs to be said about the war. It ends abruptly, like many Rosenberg poems; but what ending would be an improvement? The sense of abortiveness is essentially relevant.

BREAK OF DAY IN THE TRENCHES

Quite unlike any other trench-poem: a view of madness which itself preserves a profound sanity while understanding the impulse to a lunatic giggle. Technically the poem is masterly, in such a line as 'Hurled through still heavens' or in the disconcerting shift of the last four lines (what seems to you to be their tone? Is it well-judged?).

Wilfred Owen

Wilfred Owen was born in Shropshire in 1893. He went to London University, and was later a tutor in France, until he enlisted in October 1915. In October 1918 he was awarded the M.C. for 'conspicuous gallantry and devotion to duty'; a month later he was killed, one week before the signing of the Armistice.

His friend Siegfried Sassoon collected and published his poems in 1920. He fairly quickly became the best-known poet of the war (with the exception of Rupert Brooke, who never saw action and whose well-meaning patriotic sonnets now have an embarrassing ring), and his work was an influence upon poets of the 1930's, by its toughness and unpleasantness and its experiments with half-rhyme and onomatopoeia. Innumerable people of our century have grasped at Owen as the first poet to express, forcefully and without faltering, the protest thousands of men have wanted to express: a protest not simply against war, but against the glamourizing of war by politicians, stay-at-homes, and neurotic cripples searching for their masculinity. As that of a distinguished and loyal officer, Owen's statement was respected; and much of his poetry is deliberately founded in actual incidents, people he saw die, a meticulous painting of the appalling trenches. His methods and statements are, to say the least, straightforward, and might be called artistically naïve, but that it is clear he was aware of this risk and prepared to run it. Elaborate artistry, subtlety, indirectness were secondary to his purpose: 'the poetry is in the pity', and it was his job to speak out in terms no one could misunderstand or evade.

These principles operate in Owen's use of language. He

wants to hit us hard, and directly; and to do so he calls upon the harsher and coarser reserves of English. Ugliness is what he wants, to throw in the eyes of the glamourizers. He is a descriptive poet, and a concrete one; but his words are chosen also for their immediate emotional effect (and we may at times feel that he forces rather too crudely). His verse is mostly straightforward. The most original aspect of Owen's poetry technically is his use of half-rhyme, where the consonants of a syllable fit but the vowel does not. This enables Owen to keep the discipline and the echo-effect of rhyme, while avoiding sing-song: often the device creates a mood of grey dissatisfaction which suits admirably the poetry of ugliness.

Exposure

Our brains ache, in the merciless iced east winds that
        knive us . . .
Wearied we keep awake because the night is silent . . .
Low, drooping flares confuse our memory of the
        salient . . .
Worried by silence, sentries whisper, curious, nervous,
      But nothing happens.

Watching, we hear the mad gusts tugging on the wire,
Like twitching agonies of men among its brambles.
Northward, incessantly, the flickering gunnery rumbles,
Far off, like a dull rumour of some other war.
      What are we doing here?

The poignant misery of dawn begins to grow. . .
We only know war lasts, rain soaks, and clouds sag
        stormy.
Dawn massing in the east her melancholy army
Attacks once more in ranks on shivering ranks of grey,
      But nothing happens.

Sudden successive flights of bullets streak the silence.
Less deathly than the air that shudders black with snow,
With sidelong flowing flakes that flock, pause, and renew;
We watch them wandering up and down the wind's
        nonchalance,
      But nothing happens.

Pale flakes with fingering stealth come feeling for our
        faces—

We cringe in holes, back on forgotten dreams, and stare,
      snow-dazed,
Deep into grassier ditches. So we drowse, sun-dozed,
Littered with blossoms trickling where the blackbird
      fusses.
    Is it that we are dying?

Slowly our ghosts drag home: glimpsing the sunk fires,
      glozed
With crusted dark-red jewels; crickets jingle there;
For hours the innocent mice rejoice: the house is theirs;
Shutters and doors, all closed: on us the doors are
      closed,—
    We turn back to our dying.

Since we believe not otherwise can kind fires burn;
Nor ever suns smile true on child, or field, or fruit.
For God's invincible spring our love is made afraid;
Therefore, not loath, we lie out here; therefore were
      born,
    For love of God seems dying.

To-night, His frost will fasten on this mud and us,
Shrivelling many hands, puckering foreheads crisp.
The burying-party, picks and shovels in their shaking
      grasp,
Pause over half-known faces. All their eyes are ice,
    But nothing happens.

Dulce et Decorum Est

Bent double, like old beggars under sacks,
Knock-kneed, coughing like hags, we cursed through
   sludge,
Till on the haunting flares we turned our backs
And towards our distant rest began to trudge.
Men marched asleep. Many had lost their boots
But limped on, blood-shod. All went lame; all blind;
Drunk with fatigue; deaf even to the hoots
Of gas-shells dropping softly behind.

Gas! GAS! Quick, boys!—An ecstasy of fumbling,
Fitting the clumsy helmets just in time;
But someone still was yelling out and stumbling
And floundering like a man in fire or lime. . .
Dim, through the misty panes and thick green light,
As under a green sea, I saw him drowning.

In all my dreams, before my helpless sight,
He plunges at me, guttering, choking, drowning.

If, in some smothering dream, you too could pace
Beside the wagon that we flung him in,
And watch the white eyes writhing in his face,
His hanging face, like a devil's sick of sin;
If you could hear, at every jolt, the blood
Come gargling from the froth-corrupted lungs
Bitter as the cud
Of vile, incurable sores on innocent tongues—
My friend, you would not tell with such high zest
To children ardent for some desperate glory,
The old Lie: Dulce et Decorum Est
Pro Patria Mori.

The Sentry

We'd found an old Boche dug-out, and he knew,
And gave us hell, for shell on frantic shell
Hammered on top, but never quite burst through.
Rain, guttering down in waterfalls of slime,
Kept slush waist-high and rising hour by hour,
And choked the steps too thick with clay to climb.
What murk of air remained stank old, and sour
With fumes of whizz-bangs, and the smell of men
Who'd lived there years, and left their curse in the den,
If not their corpses . . .
              There we herded from the blast
Of whizz-bangs, but one found our door at last,—
Buffeting eyes and breath, snuffing the candles,
And thud! flump! thud! down the steep steps came
    thumping
And sploshing the flood, deluging muck—
The sentry's body; then, his rifle, handles
Of old Boche bombs, and mud in ruck on ruck.
We dredged him up, for killed, until he whined
'O sir, my eyes—I'm blind—I'm blind, I'm blind!'
Coaxing, I held a flame against his lids
And said if he could see the least blurred light
He was not blind; in time he'd get all right.
'I can't,' he sobbed. Eyeballs, huge-bulged like squids',
Watch my dreams still; but I forgot him there
In posting next for duty, and sending a scout
To beg a stretcher somewhere, and flound'ring about
To other posts under the shrieking air.

Those other wretches, how they bled and spewed,
And one who would have drowned himself for good,—

I try not to remember these things now.
Let dread hark back for one word only: how
Half listening to that sentry's moans and jumps,
And the wild chattering of his broken teeth,
Renewed most horribly whenever crumps
Pummelled the roof and slogged the air beneath—
Through the dense din, I say, we heard him shout
'I see your light!' But ours had long died out.

Futility

Move him into the sun—
Gently its touch awoke him once,
At home, whispering of fields unsown.
Always it woke him, even in France,
Until this morning and this snow.
If anything might rouse him now
The kind old sun will know.

Think how it wakes the seeds,—
Woke, once, the clays of a cold star.
Are limbs, so dear-achieved, are sides,
Full-nerved—still warm—too hard to stir?
Was it for this the clay grew tall?
—O what made fatuous sunbeams toil
To break earth's sleep at all?

Strange Meeting

It seemed that out of battle I escaped
Down some profound dull tunnel, long since scooped
Through granites which titanic wars had groined.
Yet also there encumbered sleepers groaned,
Too fast in thought or death to be bestirred.
Then, as I probed them, one sprang up, and stared
With piteous recognition in fixed eyes,
Lifting distressful hands as if to bless.
And by his smile, I knew that sullen hall,
By his dead smile I knew we stood in Hell.
With a thousand pains that vision's face was grained;
Yet no blood reached there from the upper ground,
And no guns thumped, or down the flues made moan.
'Strange friend,' I said, 'here is no cause to mourn.'
'None,' said that other, 'save the undone years,
The hopelessness. Whatever hope is yours,
Was my life also; I went hunting wild
After the wildest beauty in the world,
Which lies not calm in eyes, or braided hair,
But mocks the steady running of the hour,
And if it grieves, grieves richlier than here.
For of my glee might many men have laughed,
And of my weeping something had been left,
Which must die now. I mean the truth untold,
The pity of war, the pity war distilled.
Now men will go content with what we spoiled,
Or, discontent, boil bloody, and be spilled.
They will be swift with swiftness of the tigress.
None will break ranks, though nations trek from
     progress.
Courage was mine, and I had mystery,
Wisdom was mine, and I had mastery:

To miss the march of this retreating world
Into vain citadels that are not walled.
Then, when much blood had clogged their chariot-
    wheels,
I would go up and wash them from sweet wells,
Even with truths that lie too deep for taint.
I would have poured my spirit without stint
But not through wounds; not on the cess of war.
Foreheads of men have bled where no wounds were.
I am the enemy you killed, my friend.
I knew you in this dark: for so you frowned
Yesterday through me as you jabbed and killed.
I parried; but my hands were loath and cold.
Let us sleep now . . .'

Notes

EXPOSURE

Some of the problems Owen's poetry presents are raised by the first two lines of the second verse. 'Watching, we hear the mad gusts tugging on the wire' seems to me an immensely expressive line: the suppressed panic in a lunatic world, the misery of the weather. The second line seems to me to make unnecessarily explicit what was implied in the personification of the first, and so to reduce its force. This sort of thing happens quite often in Owen's poetry: we must remember that he was killed at the age of 25, and would probably have trained himself to be more selective later. One can mention it here because this is the kind of weakness from which EXPOSURE in general does not suffer: one of Owen's finest achievements, it is agonizing not in explosive horror but by its nervous precision, restraint, and bald questioning. 'Is it that we are dying?'

Owen spent the desperate winter of 1916–17 in the trenches. A *salient* (line 3) is a prong or outpost in the defence lines, projecting towards the enemy. *Glozed* (verse 6) means 'studded with'—but the word is chosen for its suggestions of 'glow', and, probably, for its recollection of 'dazed', 'drowse', 'dozed', in the previous verse.

DULCE ET DECORUM EST

War is a force against life: war in the trenches quickly destroyed human dignity and beauty. Owen here deliberately shows us the human body crippled and insulted—'Bent double', 'knock-kneed', 'coughing', 'lame', 'drunk', 'blind', 'deaf', 'stumbling' . . . and so on, and worse.

The Latin motto, once a familiar tub-thumping tag, means,

'It is sweet and fitting to die for one's native-land.' This attitude above all was what Owen was attacking, and this poem is his most powerful onslaught. He took a lot of trouble over it. Note his control, by punctuation, of the verse-movement (a quick comparison of lines 5–8 and 9–14 will make the point), and the complex and powerful connotations of individual words, such as 'guttering' and 'writhing'.

THE SENTRY
Boche: German. *He* in the first line means 'the Boche', i.e. the Germans (plural).

FUTILITY
The delicacy and restraint of the first lines communicates the tenderness of an actual situation; and the way in which the verse of the second stanza is allowed to move passionately, but under control, to a climax is a masterpiece of sensitive technique. Study also the way rhyme and half-rhyme add discipline and feeling. This is Owen's most timeless, universal work: and in the long run it is a more moving complaint than his more specific, blood-and-guts shock-poems.

STRANGE MEETING
This is quite unlike any other English poem: uneven, clumsy in places, it may be, but it is a basically successful attempt to make a statement in sterner, more classical terms than Owen uses elsewhere. This poem, which is not easy to read, is superbly set to music by Benjamin Britten in his well-known *War Requiem* (where poems of Owen—FUTILITY is another—are linked with the traditional Latin of the Requiem Mass).

Robert Graves

Graves was born in 1895, and was educated at Charterhouse, in the trenches, and at Oxford. His early years are described in one of the most famous and satisfactory of all autobiographies, *Goodbye To All That*, published when he was only thirty-four. For many years now he has lived in Majorca. Graves is a professional writer, and makes his living by historical novels, classical scholarship and translation, and an occasional course of lectures; but he is firm on the point that writing poetry is what matters most to him. He has published poetry fairly regularly since young-manhood, but is not prolific. He is at pains to point out that he works very hard over his poems, revising, deleting, and eventually often withdrawing earlier work.

Robert Graves is at times almost the Peter Simple of modern literature: most twentieth-century developments in poetry seem to irritate him. (In a lecture at Cambridge in the 1950's, printed in *The Crowning Privilege*, he attempted to demolish every widely-praised twentieth-century poet in England and America—except himself). His own poems are short and mostly lyrical, though sharpened with wit and irony. In recent years he has written mostly love-poems in rather seventeenth-century modes. Graves is admirably free from false pretensions: his poems are confessedly minor, limited; and they are always polished and well-made. They make a stable point of reference in English poetry between, say, 1920 and the present day. And they have their own very original voice—eccentric, often sinister, sardonic, and at times suddenly intensely poignant and vulnerable.

Rocky Acres

This is a wild land, country of my choice,
With harsh craggy mountain moor ample and bare.
Seldom in these acres is heard any voice
But voice of cold water that runs here and there
Through rocks and lank heather growing without care.
No mice in the heath run, no song-birds fly
For fear of the buzzard that floats in the sky.

He soars and he hovers, rocking on his wings,
He scans his wide parish with a sharp eye,
He catches the trembling of small hidden things,
He tears them in pieces, dropping them from the sky;
Tenderness and pity the heart will deny,
Where life is but nourished by water and rock—
A hardy adventure, full of fear and shock.

Time has never journeyed to this lost land,
Crakeberry and heather bloom out of date,
The rocks jut, the streams flow singing on either hand,
Careless if the season be early or late,
The skies wander overhead, now blue, now slate;
Winter would be known by his cutting snow
If June did not borrow his armour also.

Yet this is my country, beloved by me best,
The first land that rose from Chaos and the Flood,
Nursing no valleys for comfort and rest,
Trampled by no shod hooves, bought with no blood.
Sempiternal country whose barrows have stood
Stronghold for demigods when on earth they go,
Terror for fat burghers on far plains below.

Sick Love

O Love, be fed with apples while you may,
And feel the sun and go in royal array,
A smiling innocent on the heavenly causeway,

Though in what listening horror for the cry
That soars in outer blackness dismally,
The dumb blind beast, the paranoiac fury:

Be warm, enjoy the season, lift your head,
Exquisite in the pulse of tainted blood,
That shivering glory not to be despised.

Take your delight in momentariness,
Walk between dark and dark—a shining space
With the grave's narrowness, though not its peace.

Lost Love

His eyes are quickened so with grief,
He can watch a grass or leaf
Every instant grow; he can
Clearly through a flint wall see,
Or watch the startled spirit flee
From the throat of a dead man.
  Across two counties he can hear
And catch your words before you speak.
The woodlouse or the maggot's weak
Clamour rings in his sad ear,
And noise so slight it would surpass
Credence—drinking sound of grass,
Worm talk, clashing jaws of moth
Chumbling holes in cloth;
The groan of ants who undertake
Gigantic loads for honour's sake
(Their sinews creak, their breath comes thin);
Whir of spiders when they spin,
And minute whispering, mumbling, sighs
Of idle grubs and flies.
  This man is quickened so with grief,
He wanders god-like or like thief
Inside and out, below, above,
Without relief seeking lost love.

Sergeant-Major Money

It wasn't our battalion, but we lay alongside it,
    So the story is as true as the telling is frank.
They hadn't one Line-officer left, after Arras,
    Except a batty major and the Colonel, who drank.

'B' Company Commander was fresh from the Depot,
    An expert on gas drill, otherwise a dud;
So Sergeant-Major Money carried on, as instructed,
    And that's where the swaddies began to sweat blood.

His Old Army humour was so well-spiced and hearty
    That one poor sod shot himself, and one lost his
        wits;
But discipline's maintained, and back in rest-billets
    The Colonel congratulates 'B' Company on their
        kits.

The subalterns went easy, as was only natural
    With a terror like Money driving the machine,
Till finally two Welshmen, butties from the Rhondda,
    Bayoneted their bug-bear in a field-canteen.

Well, we couldn't blame the officers, they relied on
        Money;
    We couldn't blame the pit-boys, their courage was
        grand;
Or, least of all, blame Money, an old stiff surviving
    In a New (bloody) Army he couldn't understand.

Warning to Children

Children, if you dare to think
Of the greatness, rareness, muchness,
Fewness of this precious only
Endless world in which you say
You live, you think of things like this:
Blocks of slate enclosing dappled
Red and green, enclosing tawny
Yellow nets, enclosing white
And black acres of dominoes,
Where a neat brown paper parcel
Tempts you to untie the string.
In the parcel a small island,
On the island a large tree,
On the tree a husky fruit.
Strip the husk and pare the rind off:
In the kernel you will see
Blocks of slate enclosed by dappled
Red and green, enclosed by tawny
Yellow nets, enclosed by white
And black acres of dominoes,
Where the same brown paper parcel—
Children, leave the string untied!
For who dares undo the parcel
Finds himself at once inside it,
On the island, in the fruit,
Blocks of slate about his head,
Finds himself enclosed by dappled
Green and red, enclosed by yellow
Tawny nets, enclosed by black
And white acres of dominoes,
With the same brown paper parcel
Still untied upon his knee.

And, if he then should dare to think
Of the fewness, muchness, rareness,
Greatness of this endless only
Precious world in which he says
He lives—he then unties the string.

It Was All Very Tidy

When I reached his place,
The grass was smooth,
The wind was delicate,
The wit well timed,
The limbs well formed,
The pictures straight on the wall;
It was all very tidy.

He was cancelling out
The last row of figures,
He had his beard tied up in ribbons,
There was no dust on his shoe,
Everyone nodded:
It was all very tidy.

Music was not playing,
There were no sudden noises,
The sun shone blandly,
The clock ticked:
It was all very tidy.

'Apart from and above all this,'
I reassured myself,

'There is now myself.'
It was all very tidy.

Death did not address me,
He had nearly done:
It was all very tidy.

They asked, did I not think
It was all very tidy?

I could not bring myself
To laugh, or untie
His beard's neat ribbons,
Or jog his elbow,
Or whistle, or sing,
Or make disturbance.
I consented, frozenly,
He was unexceptionable;
It was all very tidy.

Welsh Incident

'But that was nothing to what things came out
From the sea-caves of Criccieth yonder.'
'What were they? Mermaids? dragons? ghosts?'
'Nothing at all of any things like that.'
'What were they, then?'

       'All sorts of queer things,
Things never seen or heard or written about,
Very strange, un-Welsh, utterly peculiar
Things. Oh, solid enough they seemed to touch,
Had anyone dared it. Marvellous creation,
All various shapes and sizes and no sizes,
All new, each perfectly unlike his neighbour,
Though all came moving slowly out together.'
'Describe just one of them.'

         'I am unable.'
'What was their colour?'

      'Mostly nameless colours,
Colours you'd like to see; but one was puce
Or perhaps more like crimson, but not purplish.
Some had no colour.'

      'Tell me, had they legs?'
'Not a leg nor foot among them that I saw.'
'But did these things come out in any order?
What o'clock was it? What was the day of the week?
Who else was present? How was the weather?'
'I was coming to that. It was half-past three
On Easter Tuesday last. The sun was shining.
The Harlech Silver Band played *Marchog Jesu*
On thirty-seven shimmering instruments,
Collecting for Caernarvon's (Fever) Hospital Fund.
The populations of Pwllheli, Criccieth,
Portmadoc, Borth, Tremadoc, Penrhyndeudraeth,

Were all assembled. Criccieth's mayor addressed them
First in good Welsh and then in fluent English,
Twisting his fingers in his chain of office,
Welcoming the things. They came out on the sand,
Not keeping time to the band, moving seaward
Silently at a snail's pace. But at last
The most odd, indescribable thing of all,
Which hardly one man there could see for wonder
Did something recognizably a something.'
'Well, what?'
                    'It made a noise.'
                                        'A frightening noise?'
'No, no.'
          'A musical noise? A noise of scuffling?'
'No, but a very loud, respectable noise—
Like groaning to oneself on Sunday morning
In Chapel, close before the second psalm.'
'What did the mayor do?'
                          'I was coming to that.'

In Broken Images

He is quick, thinking in clear images;
I am slow, thinking in broken images.

He becomes dull, trusting to his clear images;
I become sharp, mistrusting my broken images.

Trusting his images, he assumes their relevance;
Mistrusting my images, I question their relevance.

Assuming their relevance, he assumes the fact;
Questioning their relevance, I question the fact.

When the fact fails him, he questions his senses;
When the fact fails me, I approve my senses.

He continues quick and dull in his clear images;
I continue slow and sharp in my broken images.

He in a new confusion of his understanding;
I in a new understanding of my confusion.

Recalling War

Entrance and exit wounds are silvered clean,
The track aches only when the rain reminds.
The one-legged man forgets his leg of wood,
The one-armed man his jointed wooden arm.
The blinded man sees with his ears and hands   5
As much or more than once with both his eyes.
Their war was fought these twenty years ago
And now assumes the nature-look of time,
As when the morning traveller turns and views
His wild night-stumbling carved into a hill.   10

What, then, was war? No mere discord of flags
But an infection of the common sky
That sagged ominously upon the earth
Even when the season was the airiest May.
Down pressed the sky, and we, oppressed, thrust   15
    out
Boastful tongue, clenched fist and valiant yard.
Natural infirmities were out of mode,
For Death was young again: patron alone
Of healthy dying, premature fate-spasm.

Fear made fine bed-fellows. Sick with delight   20
At life's discovered transitoriness,
Our youth became all-flesh and waived the mind.
Never was such antiqueness of romance,
Such tasty honey oozing from the heart.
And old importances came swimming back—   25
Wine, meat, log-fires, a roof over the head,
A weapon at the thigh, surgeons at call.
Even there was a use again for God—

A word of rage in lack of meat, wine, fire,
30   In ache of wounds beyond all surgeoning.

War was return of earth to ugly earth.
War was foundering of sublimities,
Extinction of each happy art and faith
By which the world had still kept head in air,
35   Protesting logic or protesting love,
Until the unendurable moment struck—
The inward scream, the duty to run mad.

And we recall the merry ways of guns—
Nibbling the walls of factory and church
40   Like a child, piecrust; felling groves of trees
Like a child, dandelions with a switch.
Machine-guns rattle toy-like from a hill
Down in a row the brave tin-soldiers fall:
A sight to be recalled in elder days
45   When learnedly the future we devote
To yet more boastful visions of despair.

Nightfall at Twenty Thousand Feet

A black wall from the east, toppling, arches the tall sky
    over
To drown what innocent pale western lights yet cover
Cloud banks of expired sunset; so goodbye, sweet day!
From earliest green you sprang, in green tenderly glide
    away . . .
Had I never noticed, on watch before at a humbler
    height,
That crowding through dawn's gate come night and
    dead of night?

Wm. Brazier

At the end of Tarriers' Lane, which was the street
We children thought the pleasantest in Town
Because of the old elms growing from the pavement
And the crookedness, when the other streets were straight,
[They were always at the lamp-post round the corner,
Those pugs and papillons and in-betweens,
Nosing and snuffling for the latest news]
Lived Wm. Brazier, with a gilded sign,
'Practical Chimney Sweep.' He had black hands,
Black face, black clothes, black brushes and white teeth;
He jingled round the town in a pony-trap,
And the pony's name was Soot, and Soot was black.
But the brass fittings on the trap, the shafts,
On Soot's black harness, on the black whip-butt,
Twinkled and shone like any guardsman's buttons.
Wasn't that pretty? And when we children jeered:
'Hello, Wm. Brazier! Dirty-face Wm. Brazier!'
He would crack his whip at us and smile and bellow,
'Hello, my dears!' [If he were drunk, but otherwise:
'Scum off, you damned young milliners' bastards, you!']

Let them copy it out on a pink page of their albums,
Carefully leaving out the bracketed lines.
It's an old story—f's for s's—
But good enough for them, the suckers.

The Thieves

Lovers in the act dispense
With such meum-teum sense
As might warningly reveal
What they must not pick or steal,
And their nostrum is to say:
'I and you are both away.'

After, when they disentwine
You from me and yours from mine,
Neither can be certain who
Was that I whose mine was you.
To the act again they go
More completely not to know.

Theft is theft and raid is raid
Though reciprocally made.
Lovers, the conclusion is
Doubled sighs and jealousies
In a single heart that grieves
For lost honour among thieves.

The Undead

To be the only woman alive in a vast hive of death
Is a strange predicament, granted! Innumerable zombies
With glazed eyes shuffle around at their diurnal tasks,
Keep the machines whirring, drudge idly in stores and
    bars,
Bear still-born zombie children, pack them off to school
For education in science and the dead languages,
Divert themselves with moribund travesties of living,
Lay mountainous bets on horses never seen to run,
Speed along highways in conveyor-belt automobiles
But, significantly enough, often dare overshoot
The traffic signals and *boing*! destroy themselves again,
Earning expensive funerals. (These, if at last they emerge
From the select green cemetery-plots awarded them
On their twenty-first death-days by sombre uncles and
    aunts,
Will become zombies of the second degree, reverenced
Nationwide in church or synagogue.)
                                        Nevertheless,
Let none of this daunt you, child! Accept it as your fate
To live, to love, knowingly to cause true miracles,
Nor ever to find your body possessed by a cold corpse.
For one day, as you choose an unfamiliar side-street
Keeping both eyes open, alert, not apprehensive,
You shall suddenly (this is a promise) come to a brief
    halt:
For striding towards you on the same sidewalk will
    appear
A young man with the halo of life around his head,
Will catch you reassuringly by both hands, asseverating
In phrases utterly unintelligible to a zombie·

That all is well: you are neither diseased, deranged, nor
    mistaken
But merely undead. He will name others like you, no less
    alive:
Two girls and a man, all moneyless immigrants arrived
Lately at a new necropolitan conurbation.
'Come with me, girl, and join them! The dead, you will
    observe,
Can exercise no direct sanctions against the living
And therefore doggedly try to omit them from all the
    records.
Still, they cannot avoid a certain morbid fascination
With what they call our genius. They will venture
    questions
But never wait for an answer—being doubtless afraid
That it will make their ears burn, or their eyes prick with
    tears—
Nor can they countermand what orders we may issue.'

Nod your assent, go with him, do not even return to
    pack!
When five live people room together, each rates as a
    million—
But encourage the zombies to serve you, the honest
    creatures,
For though one cannot ameliorate their way of death
By telling them true stories or singing them real songs,
They will feel obscurely honoured by your warm
    presence.

Notes

SICK LOVE

The theme (and the diction of the first line) is traditional: death will come soon, make the most of physical life. 'Take your delight in momentariness'—the doctrine of the nineteenth-century Aesthetic writers: the beauty of things is enhanced by knowledge of their mortality. This poem seems to me a perfect example of a revived tradition: the verse and diction are alive, fresh, yet richly reminiscent of the great poetry of the past.

LOST LOVE

Quickened means made keener, more alive. What love the man has lost we are not told, but the loss has given him an uncanny nervous sensitivity to the world about him. This is a completely original poem, which it is hard to relate to any other. The strain of eeriness in Graves here emerges at its most delicate. This is a fine poem to speak aloud, observing the see-sawing verse and the onomatopoeias of the strange central section.

WARNING TO CHILDREN

The warning is against excessive philosophical puzzling: the more one seeks to understand the nature of reality, the more unreal things become. One can only stand so much. Many Continental writers this century have expressed a claustrophobia as they untie the parcels of our perception and thought. This sober English voice seems to say that there are some questions it does not pay to ask.

Study carefully the wording of the apparent repetitions.

IT WAS ALL VERY TIDY

One may think one has read this poem several times before, written by, say, Thomas Hardy, or Walter de la Mare. But Graves's imagination is entirely original and unpredictable; and that makes the poem unusually frightening. 'The wit well timed', for example: this seems utterly unrelated to the context, yet it is phrased so precisely and fits so neatly by rhythm and assonance ('the wind . . .' 'the wit . . .'), that one feels there must be a logic one does not perceive. The ribbons tying up Death's beard? . . . It is an Alice-in-Wonderland world, equally hard and unsympathetic. Part of the point probably is that Death is not as expected and is not intelligible. And as long as the poem exists Death does not turn and address the speaker (who retains a consciousness of himself): but after the poem ends. . . ?

WELSH INCIDENT

The Graves eeriness mixes with the Graves mischief. The poem needs to be read in an earnest explanatory Welsh voice.

RECALLING WAR

The simile in lines 9–10 seems to me exceptionally exact and appropriate: as similes should, it sums up so much about the war which it would be awkward and laborious to express straightforwardly. The poem in general is phrased with much sarcastic precision: in theme and handling it is perhaps Graves's most substantial achievement.

20–2. compare SICK LOVE (page 128).

24. possibly a reference to the most popular of the poets killed in the First World War, Rupert Brooke, whose poems celebrate simple fleshly gratifications, including the ingratiating line 'And is there honey still for tea?'

31–7. a rare moment of large-scale abstraction in Graves. As with some of the love-poems, there is perhaps a debt to Yeats in style. Note the punch of the hard word 'struck' after the mellifluous 'noble' lines preceding, and the deliberate crudity of 'scream' and 'run mad'.

38. the word *merry* is perhaps the most telling in the whole poem. The underlying theme throughout has been that archaic ideas of chivalric battle, pageantry, glory, were partly to blame for the horror of the war: see lines 16, 18–20 ('young again', 'healthy', 'fine bed-fellows'), 22, 26–7 (cruelly mocked by 28–30). *Merry* fits with this, and also anticipates the idea of lines 39–43: that our warfare was like the selfish irresponsible play of a child.

44–6. How hopeful is the tone?

WM. BRAZIER
An attack on sentimentalizing of childhood or poverty. If the bracketed lines are left out the poem becomes a jolly Christmas-card-ish anecdote suitable for albums. The last two lines are pure Gravesian mischief.

THE THIEVES
A witty love-lyric of a seventeenth-century kind. Lovers are two individualities, who at times feel themselves, and want to be, one. The poem is about the attempt entirely to share and trust another person: Graves warns that this is never really possible.

THE UNDEAD
A fairly recent poem commenting forcefully and characteristically on twentieth-century American society.

ACKNOWLEDGEMENTS

Acknowledgements are due to the following for permission to publish copyright material: Laurence Pollinger Ltd. and the Estate of the late Mrs. Frieda Lawrence for poems from *The Complete Poems of D. H. Lawrence*, published by William Heinemann Ltd.; Faber & Faber Ltd. for the poems by Ezra Pound and T. S. Eliot; the Literary Executors of Isaac Rosenberg and Chatto & Windus Ltd. for the poems from *The Collected Poems of Isaac Rosenberg*; Mr. Harold Owen and Chatto & Windus Ltd. for the poems from *The Collected Poems of Wilfred Owen*; and Mr. Robert Graves for his poems, published by Cassell & Co. Ltd. in *Collected Poems 1965*, *Collected Poems 1959* and *More Poems 1961*.